OLYMPIC CHAMPION

NEERAJ CHOPRA

Sanjay Dudhane

Olympic Champion
Neeraj Chopra

Sakal Media Pvt. Ltd.
595, Budhwar Peth,
Pune– 411002, India

www.sakalmediagroup.com
sakalpublications.com
sakalprakashan@esakal.com

First Edition: 2024

ISBN: 978-81-975255-9-9

Translated by: Nupur J.
Edited by: Manjula Shukla
Cover Design: Sakal Publications

Printed in India by Sakal Media Pvt. Ltd.

To the Japanese friends,

Ajay Doke and Rahul Bapat.

Contents...

Preface

For many years, like a parched bird waiting for rain, I eagerly awaited the moment to witness India winning an Olympic gold medal in person. That was why I insisted on attending the Olympics for the third consecutive time. I first participated in the grand 2012 London Olympics. In London, India secured six medals, but no gold. I was fortunate to attend the 2016 Rio Olympics as well, but the national anthem did not resonate there either. Finally, the moment arrived at the 2021 Tokyo Olympics, in the land of the rising sun, Japan.

The historic javelin throw by the valiant Neeraj Chopra and the stadium, electrified with the national anthem, still gives me goosebumps. In Tokyo, I had the blissful experience of witnessing Neeraj's unprecedented golden triumph, and my heartfelt desire of seeing Indian athletes win bronze, silver, and gold at the Olympics was fulfilled. I was a witness to the historic achievement of India's 15 Olympic medals—9 bronze, 5 silver, and 1 gold—and

I provided direct coverage of this monumental success. Even today, I find it hard to believe my good fortune. I had seen the Golden Fish, Michael Phelps, and the fastest sprinter, Usain Bolt, win gold medals at the Olympics, but Neeraj's gold medal ceremony is a cherished memory.

In recent years, the hectic lifestyle, and the demands of reporting for a news channel had pushed my book writing to the back burner. However, Neeraj's golden triumph reignited my passion for writing. On my way back home from Tokyo, I resolved to pen down Neeraj's biography. I had hoped to publish the book within a year, but it took three years as I struggled to find the right words. Finally, in the Olympic year of 2024, the writing was completed. I am overjoyed that this new book is being published by Sakal Prakashan.

My writing journey, which began with the biography of India's first Olympic medallist, Khashaba Jadhav, has now reached the modern-day Olympic hero, Neeraj. Just as Khashaba's story inspired many athletes, I pray that this biography will serve as a motivational mantra, not only for athletes but for everyone.

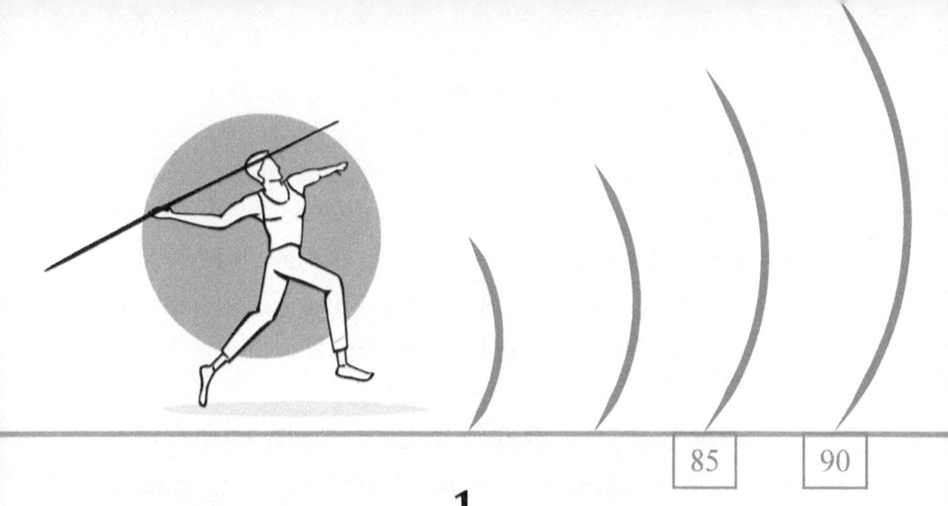

1

The Dawn of a Golden Era

"When the desire for success keeps you awake at night,
When nothing feels good except hard work,
When you don't feel tired even after working continuously,
Understand that you are about to create a new history of success."

- Neeraj Chopra

Following London and Rio, I was fortunate to participate in the grand spectacle of the Tokyo Olympics for the third consecutive time. Driven by the desire to hear the national anthem, I braved the challenges of COVID and travelled to Tokyo, as India had not won a gold medal in England or Brazil. Finally, in Japan, I witnessed that golden moment with my own eyes. I was a witness to Neeraj Chopra's historic javelin throw, an extraordinary and exhilarating moment. It epitomized the essence of the Olympics, unveiling its grandeur, vastness, and the extremes of success and failure. In the land of the rising sun, Japan, India made its mark with a historic performance, winning 1 gold, 2 silver, and 4 bronze medals.

This was the best performance in the 125-year history of the Olympics. Witnessing the national anthem being sung on the Olympic victory podium in athletics for the first time, thanks to Neeraj Chopra, filled me with immense pride. The sight of Neeraj throwing the javelin 87.58 metres towards the sky, taking the victory lap with the tricolour in hand, and our chants of 'Bharat Mata ki Jai' echoing in the stadium still give me chills. A new era had dawned. As the golden chapter of the Olympics concluded, my journey to Tokyo turned out to be a cherry on top of the cake.

On Saturday, August 7, 2021, we Indians were making our way to the main athletics stadium in Tokyo. All Indian eyes were not just on the thrill of the athletics race but were fixed on whether Neeraj's javelin would cross the medal mark. In the Tokyo Games, 125 Indian athletes across 18 sports had given their best. Until the last day, no gold medal had been won. Mirabai and Ravi Kumar had achieved silver success, while P.V. Sindhu, Lovlina, Bajrang, and the Indian hockey team had earned bronze medals. But the elusive gold still had not adorned India's name. Only one warrior was left on the field now — the valiant Neeraj Satishkumar Chopra. The sun had set, and it was twilight.

In the bright spotlight, the introduction parade of the world's top 12 javelin throwers began. In his blue tracksuit, the "Blue Tiger" Neeraj greeted the world. His face and body language declared, "Yes, I will be the champion of this battlefield." Wearing jersey number 2297, Neeraj was the second among the twelve to throw the javelin. Andrian from the small European country of Moldova initiated the contest with the first throw. Then, the twenty-three-year-old, Neeraj, from India prepared for his first throw. He tightened the belt around his waist. Despite the rain making the track wet, he took a powerful run-up and launched the javelin into the sky. It landed like a bullet on the green field beyond the track, right in front of the press box. The screen displayed an impressive distance of 87.03 metres.

This throw itself sent a message to the world that this was the golden line, beyond which no one would go, "Today is my day. I, alone, will be beyond 87." As the famous dialogue by Amitabh

Bachchan in the movie "Kaalia" goes, "We are the ones who never stand behind anyone, wherever we stand, the line begins there," Neeraj truly embodied this spirit. He came, he saw, he conquered. With his very first attempt in the javelin throw at the Tokyo Olympics, Neeraj threw an astounding 87.03 metres, heralding the arrival of a new king on the global stage. This first attempt was enough to eclipse the efforts of the other 11 competitors over the next six tries. Not even the reigning world champion, Johannes Vetter of Germany, could surpass it.

Before the start of the Olympics in 2021, Johannes Vetter had a stronghold on javelin throwing. The chant "Vetter, Vetter" for the Tokyo javelin champion had already begun in Germany. Vetter had crossed the 90-metre mark seven times, which was why no one took Neeraj seriously before the Olympics. Even after Neeraj topped the qualification round in his first attempt in Tokyo, he did not receive much attention. In the Olympic special on News 18 Lokmat, I had predicted that it would be a golden conclusion and that Army man, Neeraj, would create golden history. That moment was now close.

Due to the rain, the track was wet, and as Johannes Vetter threw his javelin, he faltered against Neeraj's confident performance. Vetter slipped on the wet runway, resulting in his best throw being only 82.52 metres in the first round. He could not make it to the final eight athletes who got six attempts. The reigning world champion, Vetter's last two of three attempts were technically disqualified, ending his challenge. By then, the world had already sensed that Neeraj was on his way to becoming a medallist.

Neeraj's historic second attempt in the javelin throw still plays out like a thrilling movie scene in my mind. On the damp track, Neeraj focused all his strength into the 2.7-metre javelin. Holding the javelin in his right hand, he sprinted forward and launched it just four and a half feet before the final line. The javelin soared like a missile, destined to strike precisely where intended. As soon as the javelin left his hand, Neeraj raised his arms in celebration, knowing it was a historic throw. The javelin landed firmly at 87.58 metres, surpassing the mark set by his first throw. Sharp, powerful, and fast, it pierced the ground beyond 87 metres.

The moment was filled with immense joy, both in the air and on the ground. A golden smile spread across Neeraj's face. Stepping out of our roles as journalists, we became fans of Neeraj, chanting, "Bharat Mata ki Jai," in unison.

While the women's 10,000 metres final was in progress, the javelin throw competition was also taking place. The athletics field was bustling with activity, but nothing seemed to faze Neeraj. He remained calm and composed. After his first throw, a smile spread across his face. His confidence soared after the second throw, solidifying his gold medal position. However, the competition was not over yet; four rounds remained. The Olympics were unpredictable; anything could happen. In the morning session, Aditi was close to winning silver in the final round of golf but missed her penultimate shot, dropping to fourth place. Just a few hours before Neeraj's historic moment, wrestler Bajrang Punia, who had hoped for gold, had to settle for bronze. But the unwavering confidence in Neeraj's javelin throw was evident. The valiant Neeraj had luck on his side. Johannes Vetter, who could have turned the tables, was not among the final eight. India was assured of a medal; the only question was its colour. The capable Czech athletes, Vadlejch and Veselý, were still in the competition, posing a potential challenge.

From his very first attempt, no one could surpass Neeraj's mark of 87 metres. That day belonged to Neeraj. It belonged to all 1.25 billion Indians. Leaving behind competitors from Germany, Russia, Sweden, Bulgaria, Finland, Belarus, and Pakistan, Neeraj maintained a golden lead right from his first throw. Ultimately, the contest for medals unfolded only between Neeraj and the Czech athletes Vadlejch and Veselý in the last two attempts. In his fifth attempt, Vadlejch threw his season's best of 86.67 metres, challenging Neeraj. However, as Vadlejch and Veselý both fouled in their final throws, Neeraj's name was etched on the gold medal. Even before his last javelin throw, the rise of a new Olympic champion had already been heralded. Although he could not record his personal best of 88 metres in the end, Neeraj's second attempt had already ensured that the Indian tricolour would fly high in glory.

The thrill still sends shivers down my spine. Overcoming a shoulder injury, Neeraj soared like a phoenix. It was an extraordinary moment for the nation. As soon as Neeraj threw the javelin, it heralded the dawn of a golden era for India. Holding the tricolour, Neeraj took a victory lap. He even responded to my congratulations by raising his hand. Soon after, the victory podium was adorned, and medals were awarded to Veselý, Vadlejch, and Neeraj. Following the COVID-19 protocols, Neeraj adorned himself with the gold medal, which was followed by chants of "Bharat Mata Ki Jai" and "Vande Mataram." As the Czech Republic's flags were raised, the tune of India's national anthem filled the air. It was a moment so overwhelming that I could never forget it. The packed stadium stood in salute to the Indian tricolour — a sight to behold.

None of Neeraj's competitors could surpass his performance of 87.58 metres. In the main Olympic stadium, where only athletics events are held, the Indian tricolour had never flown in its 125-year history. Legendary athletes like Milkha Singh and P.T. Usha had reached as close as fourth place. Milkha Singh had a fervent wish to see the tricolour hoisted in this stadium, a dream that remained unfulfilled. Ultimately, by dedicating his gold medal to the late Milkha Singh, Neeraj not only displayed profound patriotism but also immortalized it beyond the field. Neeraj established a dominion of Indian soil in the arena and became an inspirational sports figure for the entire nation. His success story in Tokyo became the stuff of legends.

> **Olympics 2020 Javelin throw results:**
>
> **Gold** - Neeraj Chopra (India)
> **Silver** - Vadlejch (Czech Republic)
> **Bronze** - Veselý (Czech Republic)

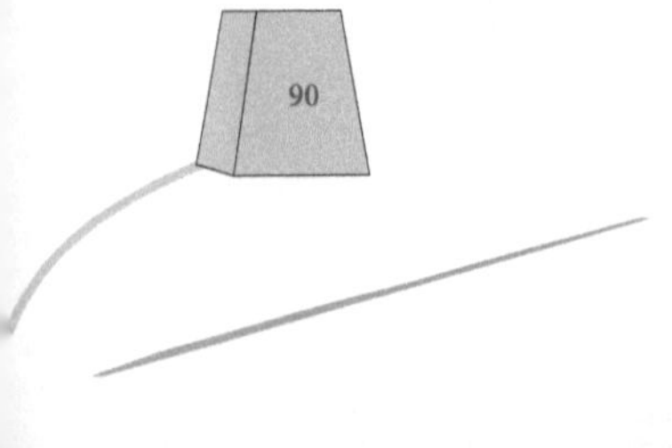

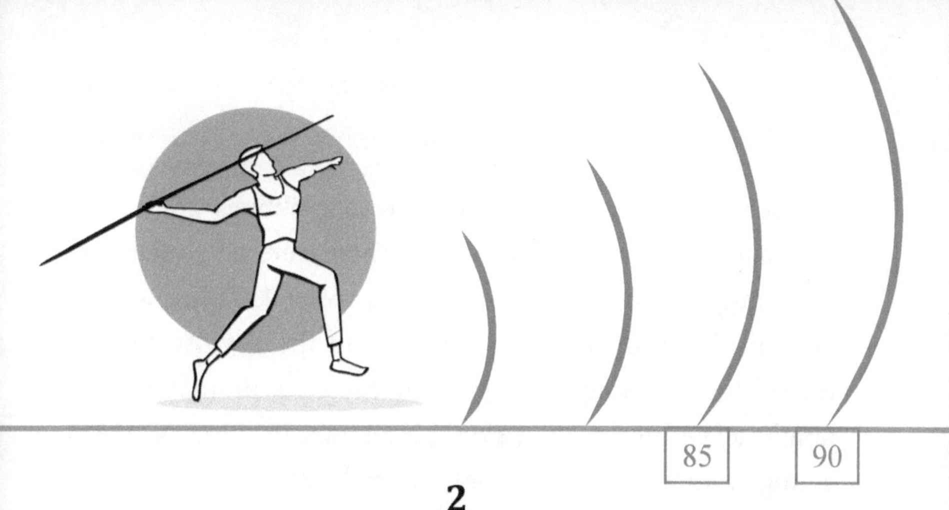

2

The Hefty Head of the Village

Neeraj was quite chubby during his childhood. When he wore a *kurta-pajama*, he resembled the leaders of his village. Consequently, he earned the nickname 'Mota Sarpanch', the hefty village head. At that time, no one imagined Neeraj would become a javelin thrower. The Chopra family was constantly thinking about how to reduce his weight.

The Chopra family originally hailed from Maharashtra, from the Maratha community. Following the historic battle of Panipat, the Chopras settled in Panipat, Haryana. Neeraj was born on December 24, 1997, in the village of Khandra, Panipat district, to Satish Kumar Chopra. His mother, Saroj Devi, doted on Neeraj and his two sisters from their childhood. Neeraj was the darling of the family. His stout physique made him look like a sumo wrestler, and there was always talk in the household about sending him to a wrestling arena.

Satish Kumar Chopra, along with his four siblings, continues to reside in the village of Khandra. There were no athletes in the family. As soon as morning broke, Neeraj's father would head to the fields and work throughout the day. As Neeraj turned ten, his weight continued to increase, prompting the family to enforce a strict exercise regime. In 2010, Neeraj's younger uncle, Bhim Chopra, started taking him out for morning runs. Gradually, Neeraj also began visiting the gym with him. One day, they took him to the stadium in Panipat.

Shivaji Stadium in Panipat, located about 15 kilometres from Neeraj's village, Khandra, became his new athletic ground. He started frequenting the gym there, running to reduce

his weight. He began to find more joy on the field and in the gym than in his school textbooks. The exercise, particularly running, transformed his physique significantly.

Shivaji Stadium in Panipat was primarily an athletics venue. It was the only major sports arena in the bustling city of Panipat, catering to the local athletes. Training for various athletics disciplines such as running, long jump, high jump, shot put, and javelin throw was conducted here. Exhausted from running, Neeraj would curiously watch the athletes engaged in these sports. He was particularly fascinated by the javelin throwers, mimicking their actions. The sight of the javelin soaring through the air and piercing the ground captivated him, and he often paused during his exercises to observe it closely.

One day, while working out in the gym with his uncle, Bhim Chopra, Neeraj met Jayveer Chaudhary, a javelin thrower from the nearby village of Bhajhol. Neeraj had seen Jayveer practicing javelin throw several times. When he encountered Jayveer, young Neeraj curiously asked if javelin throw was a sport. Jayveer happily affirmed that it indeed was. Hearing this, Neeraj returned to his workout, but the fascination with the javelin had firmly planted itself in his mind.

After Diwali in 2010, while exercising at Shivaji Stadium, Neeraj saw some athletes throwing the javelin. This reignited his thoughts about the sport. When he returned home, he met Jayveer again and declared, "Sir, I want to learn this sport." That same day, he discussed his new interest in javelin throw with his family. His father, Satish Kumar, and uncle, Bhim, were quite surprised but offered no resistance. They encouraged him, "Go to the field. Exercise as much as you need. Pursue whatever sport you like," blessing their beloved son with their full support.

Filled with immense joy, Neeraj went to Shivaji Stadium the very next day and began his training in javelin throw under Jayveer Chaudhary, who became his first coach. Neeraj learned the basics of javelin throw from Coach Jayveer. Holding the long javelin for the first time was a thrilling experience for Neeraj; the javelin, larger than his own height, was of Indian make. During the first week, he was trained on how to hold the javelin properly as part of his initial lessons, which complemented his running exercises. As he learned to grip the javelin firmly, he began to practice the throwing action while running.

Those were days full of activity. Every day, the thirteen-year-old stout Neeraj would set out from Khandra village towards Panipat for his javelin throw training at the Sports Authority of India's facility. He always seemed to be in a hurry to everyone around him, rushing home from BVN Public School to change out of his uniform and head straight to Panipat. Since buses arrived hourly, he often found himself anxiously waiting at the bus stand. Once in Panipat, he would either walk or run the last one and a half kilometres to the training ground. The return journey, especially after an exhausting practice session, was even more challenging. It often got late, and he would find himself travelling back in the dark, sometimes hitching rides on a bike or a tractor. Occasionally, it got very late, but Neeraj never complained. He relished the daily routine of physical exertion. Some of his peers from the village also joined him, sharing the rigorous journey.

After learning the basics from Jayveer, one day Neeraj was ready to showcase his javelin skills. Running from a distance, he launched the javelin into the air with a powerful throw. His very first javelin landed impressively beyond 25 metres. Both Coach Jayveer and Neeraj's faces lit up with joy. It was the rise of Neeraj, the javelin thrower. Seeing Neeraj's natural gift in this sport, Coach Jayveer was astonished. Neeraj had thrown further than even the senior athletes. His performance in his very first throw indicated that he was destined to become a champion one day.

Neeraj's training sessions at Shivaji Stadium in Panipat would often continue until late evening. This made it a challenge for him to return home late at night. As a result, after a few months, he decided to stay at the sports hostel in Panipat. While learning javelin throw from Jayveer, he also picked up techniques from senior athletes. Initially, everyone pooled money together to buy three javelins. Later, they also received locally made javelins from the government. Once, a bronze javelin Neeraj was using broke. In Panipat, there were more athletes than javelins available. When the seniors learned about the broken javelin, they scolded Neeraj, expressing their frustration that the sports department would not provide new javelins and questioned him as to how they were supposed to practice. Neeraj sat quietly, like Hanuman, without responding. However, that day, he resolved to do something so that he would never fall short of expensive javelins for practice.

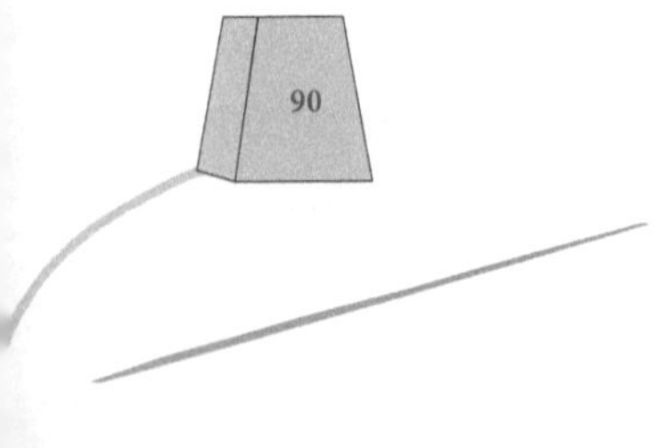

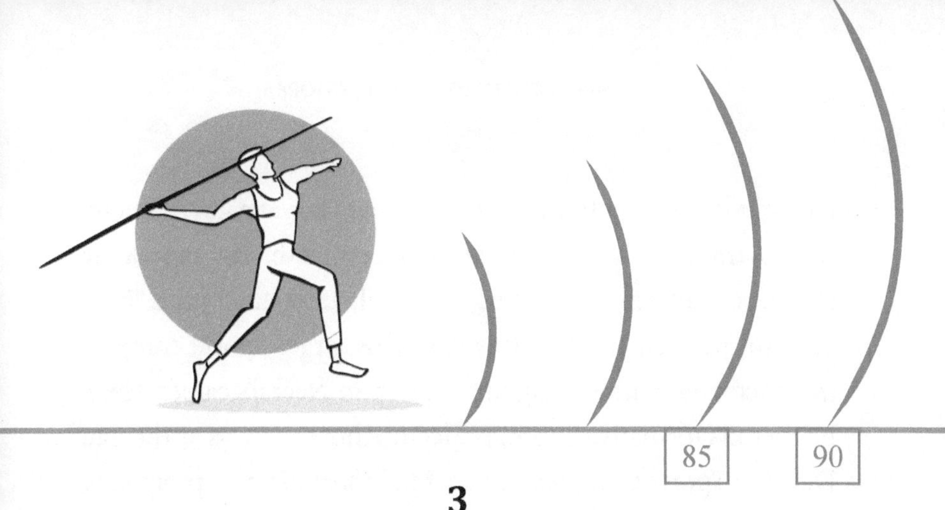

3

The Sports Facility in Panchkula

Neeraj started sweating it out every evening at Shivaji Stadium, yet his weight was not decreasing. Seeing his passion for javelin throw, his family decided to enrol him in an academy in Panchkula, a decision that would prove to be a turning point in his life.

In Panipat, Neeraj had already established a connection with the sport of javelin throw. His first coach, Jayveer Chaudhary, was also active in the sport at that time. Together, with a few other colleagues who were aiming to enhance their skills, the mentor and disciple decided to move to the sports academy in Panchkula.

In 2011, Neeraj bid farewell to his parents and relatives and travelled for four hours to reach the sports complex in

Panchkula. This centre, sponsored by the Haryana government, was a training hub for various sports. Athletes practicing athletics, badminton, boxing, football, basketball, and judo can still be seen there to this day. This larger sports complex in Panchkula marked a significant step in Neeraj's career. Here, he met his formative coach, Nadeem Ahmed. It was at the Tau Devi Lal Sports Complex in Panchkula that Neeraj's promising journey was set to begin.

Having moved away from home to pursue a career in athletics, Neeraj quickly adapted to his new environment in Panchkula. A fair-skinned young teenager of just under thirteen, Neeraj's noble demeanour caught the eye of Coach Aseem Ahmed during their very first meeting. His rigorous training days began at dawn. Along with other athletes, Neeraj would run on the Shivalik Hills in Panchkula. He spent the mornings

training with long-distance runners and dedicated his evenings to perfecting his javelin throw.

In Panipat, Neeraj had taken basic javelin throw training with senior athletes. This foundation allowed Coach Ahmed to focus on enhancing Neeraj's strength and endurance as soon as he arrived in Panchkula. Ahmed tailored a rigorous workout regimen for him. He observed Neeraj's resilience in running tirelessly on the mountains and his consistency in the basic javelin throw practice sessions every evening. Neeraj would sit beside the coach with a small notebook, diligently noting down the nuances of the sport. Coach Ahmed quickly realized that a unique chemistry was developing between them, as Neeraj absorbed every lesson with keen interest.

At that time, Haryana had only two international standard synthetic athletic tracks, one of which was in Panchkula. The combination of a state-of-the-art facility, expert coaching, and convenient residential arrangements created an ideal environment for cultivating successful athletes, allowing Neeraj to focus entirely on his training. His journey toward becoming a competitive javelin thrower began in Panchkula. His routine included complementary exercises in the morning, ample rest in the afternoon, and technical training in the evenings, which gradually reduced his weight. This progress brought great joy to his family, and hence, no one asked him to come home to study or work in the fields anymore. Either his father or his cousins would visit him once a month, and his mother never forgot to send a box filled with goodies with them. The Chopra family was now resolute in their decision to support Neeraj's athletic career.

Months passed and Ahmed focused on improving Neeraj's throwing technique. He mastered the art of making angular strides while sprinting with the javelin, which significantly aided the force and smooth landing of the throws. The technique of running in javelin-throw mode needed to be precise. Neeraj's technique was gradually refined. Initially, he would take two long strides for the throw, then he moved to three, and eventually, he could take five strides before executing an accurate throw. Day by day, he improved his throws by running at full capacity. The beginning of the run, in javelin throw, is as crucial as the final positioning, known as the landing. Perfecting a javelin throw is a significant art, and Neeraj diligently worked to master it.

As the days progressed, Neeraj's trajectory of progress steeply climbed. For athletes, it is essential to find the right mentor at the right turn in their journey, and Neeraj was fortunate in this regard. Just as Bharat Ratna Sachin Tendulkar and India's first Olympic medallist Khashaba Jadhav had found expert coaches at crucial times, which helped them become great athletes, Neeraj too was blessed with outstanding guidance. As his career blossomed, he received increasingly sophisticated coaching, enhancing his skills and performance.

Initially in Panipat, Neeraj received basic training from Jayveer. Later, in Panchkula, Nadeem Ahmed shaped his foundational skills. At the camp in Patiala, Army man Kashinath Naik and Gary Calvert transformed him into an international medallist. Werner Daniels further developed his technique for longer throws, while Klaus Bartonietz brought him to the doorstep of the Olympics with classical biotechnique methods. Ultimately, Uwe Hohn moulded him into an Olympic champion. Over a decade, seven coaches enriched Neeraj's career leading to the Olympic gold.

When Neeraj clinched the Olympic medal, he did not forget to express his gratitude to all his coaches. While many athletes might forget their first coach, Neeraj excelled in paying homage to his mentors. After securing the medal, he shared the significance of this lineage of coaching with us journalists, highlighting the pivotal roles each played in his journey.

Neeraj's Lineage of Coaches:
- Jayveer Chaudhary
- Nadeem Ahmed
- Kashinath Naik
- Gary Calvert
- Werner Daniels
- Klaus Bartonietz
- Uwe Hohn

Neeraj Chopra with Coach Uwe Hohn

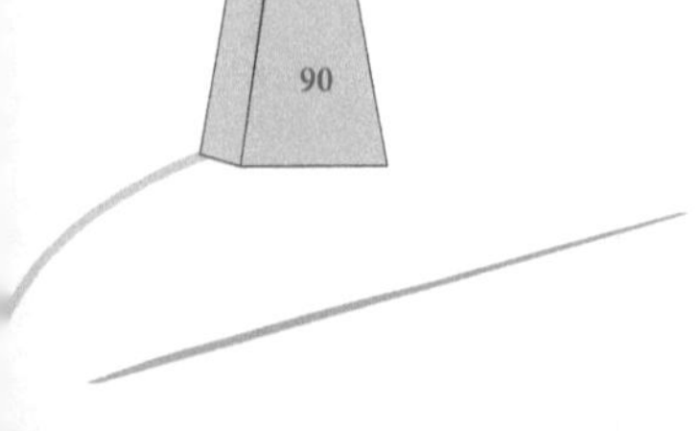

4

The Determination to Win

Haryana is known as a powerhouse in India's sports sector. The state's cricketer, Kapil Dev, led the country to its first cricket World Cup victory in 1983, a sport that enjoys peak popularity in the country. Olympic medallists like Sushil Kumar, Sakshi Malik, and Geeta Phogat—who became a household name through the film "Dangal"—along with hundreds of Commonwealth and Asian Games gold medallists have all emerged from Haryana. The state is particularly known as a factory for wrestling and boxing. Previously, athletics, especially javelin throw, did not have prominence in Haryana. Now, javelin throw is prominently mentioned as a core Indian sport within Haryana's sporting tradition. Neeraj was the first to conjure the magic of an Olympic gold medal from the soil of Haryana in this sport.

While Haryana was traditionally known for producing wrestlers and boxers, Neeraj chose to wield the javelin instead. Unlike the common advice to pursue cricket or wrestling, nobody suggested these options to him. After starting his training in Panipat, Neeraj became fully engaged in javelin throw training in Panchkula. His performance, which started from throws of 25 metres, had surpassed 50 metres by 2011.

The year 2012 marked the arrival of the Olympics, set to take place in the ever-vibrant city of London. During this global sporting spectacle, Haryana's Sushil Kumar clinched a medal for India for the second consecutive time, energizing athletes back home. This achievement inspired a renewed vigour among the athletes in Haryana. The state government also decided to enhance the facilities and provide better sports equipment to its athletes, boosting their training infrastructure.

New sports equipment, including foreign-made javelins, arrived at the Panchkula complex. Practicing diligently with the new javelins, Neeraj managed to maintain throws around the 68 to 70 metres mark—a distance unprecedented in the under-16 category. The organizers in Haryana were thrilled. The state had discovered a new champion, and it did not take long for everyone to realize that this champion was not just a state hero but had the potential to be a national icon.

After the Olympics, the frenzy of state and national competitions began in India. The state-level athletics competition was announced, and Neeraj shone in his very first competition, securing a gold medal. Winning the state competition prepared him for the junior national championships. With rigorous training over one and a half years, having surpassed the 68-metre mark, Neeraj was now eyeing a national medal. Mandeep Kumar, who had secured the silver medal in javelin throw at the under-16 junior competitions for Haryana, was selected alongside Neeraj.

In October 2012, the Junior National Championships were announced. This event would take place in Lucknow. From October 27 to October 31, 2012 athletes from across the country were set to converge on the capital of Uttar Pradesh to showcase their talents. The 28th National Junior Athletics Championship was inaugurated at the Guru Gobind Singh Sports College. Competitions in three age categories—under 20, under 18, and under 16—for boys and girls in races, throws, and jumps were expected to highlight emerging national talents.

Many athletes from the Panchkula sports complex had been selected to participate in the national competitions. Neeraj, along with the team of athletes from Haryana, arrived in Uttar Pradesh's capital. On the opening day of the competition, October 27, Neeraj was scheduled to compete in his javelin throw event during the afternoon session. Before his event, athletes in the under-20 and under-18 categories would test their fortunes in javelin throw.

The first session for the under-20 category at the competition was dominated by javelin thrower Rajesh Kumar from the host state, Uttar Pradesh. In his fourth attempt, Rajesh Kumar set a national record with a remarkable throw of 80.14 metres, securing the gold medal. Following this, in the afternoon session for the under-18 category, another athlete from Uttar Pradesh, Abhishek, showcased an impressive performance, throwing 73.46 metres.

With records being set in the under-20 and under-18 categories, there was heightened anticipation for what the under-16 competitors would achieve. After 1 P.M., fifteen competitors from across the country readied themselves. There was a palpable tension among athletes from host Uttar Pradesh, Haryana, Maharashtra, Madhya Pradesh, Rajasthan, Uttarakhand, Tamil Nadu, Andhra Pradesh, and Punjab. Notable among the prospective winners were Ashish Kumar from Uttar Pradesh, Bharat Patel from Madhya Pradesh, and from Haryana, Neeraj Chopra and Mandeep Kumar, who were very promising.

At the Junior National Athletics Championships held in Lucknow in 2012, athletes from Tamil Nadu, Maharashtra, Bihar, and Punjab were unable to reach the 50-metre mark. However, in his debut at the national competition, Neeraj's javelin sailed to 67.19 metres in the first round. He was the only athlete to throw the longest distance right from the start, ensuring his gold medal. As the second round began, Neeraj, with a powerful stride, launched the 700-gram javelin even farther. The distance was measured at 68.46 metres, setting a new national record. The announcement echoed through the speakers at Guru Govind Singh Sports College, which reverberated with cheers for Neeraj. Both he and his coaches beamed with joy, marking a record-setting debut in his first attempt in national competitions.

The 2012 Junior Athletics National Championship became historic. Athletes in all age categories had performed record-breaking feats. It was Neeraj's first competition, marking a new era in Indian athletics. These athletes were poised to grace international arenas, qualify for the Olympics, and claim global medals following their national records.

At the Junior National Athletics Championship held in Lucknow, the presence of P.T. Usha, affectionately known as the "Payyoli Express", added notable glamour. Usha, a distinguished figure in Indian athletics, narrowly missed an Olympic medal by a fraction of a second at the 1984 Los Angeles Olympics, finishing fourth. Similarly, Milkha Singh had also narrowly missed a medal at the 1960 Olympics, losing by a mere fraction of a second in a photo finish. For many years, these were considered the closest India had come to winning Olympic medals in athletics. The event in Lucknow was seen as a beacon of hope, a platform where the unfulfilled dreams of legends like P.T. Usha and Milkha Singh might find a new champion to realize them.

> ### 2012 Junior Athletics National Championship
>
> **Event**: Javelin Throw
> **Gold Medal**: Neeraj Chopra, Haryana
> **Performance**: Throws of 67.19 metres, 68.52 metres, and 63.52 metres.

This championship was a pivotal moment, not just for Neeraj Chopra but also for Indian athletics, heralding the rise of a new star capable of achieving international success and potentially fulfilling the longstanding aspirations of Indian track and field sportspersons.

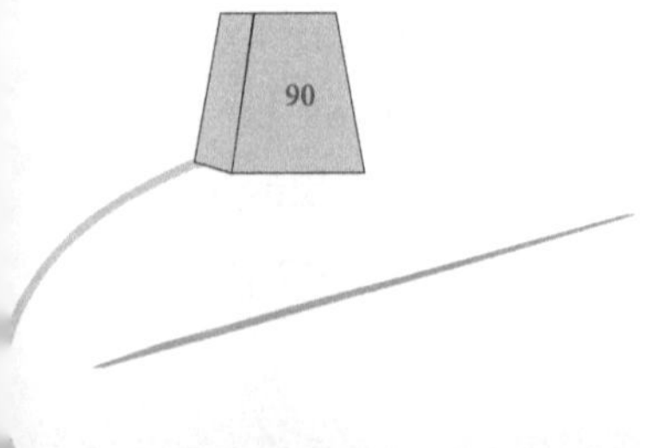

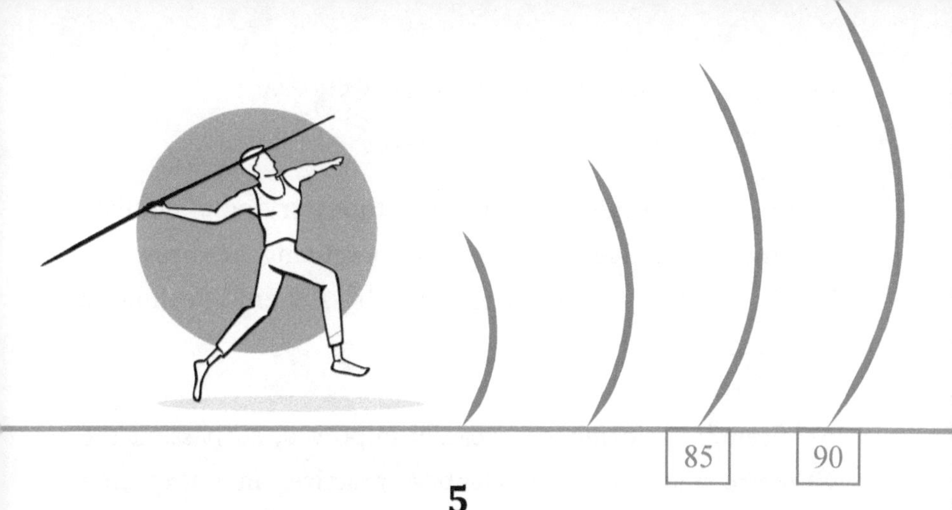

5

Setback in Ukraine

After his triumphant performance in Lucknow, Neeraj became a celebrated figure throughout Haryana. His achievement of setting a national record in the under-16 category brought great pride to the Haryana team. Neeraj was lauded across the sports community in Haryana, and even his family celebrated by indulging him with his favourite dessert, *churma*. When he returned home with the gold medal, it was a moment of great celebration, and the local newspapers, filled with stories of his performance, added to the community's pride.

Within a week, Neeraj returned to Panchkula from his village, Khanda. The recent medal had fuelled his training enthusiasm even more. He sometimes watched videos of international athletes to learn from their techniques. His friend Parmdarshan had downloaded a video of Jan Železný, the champion javelin thrower from the Czech Republic.

Neeraj watched this video multiple times, trying to emulate Železný's style. He was diligently practicing to throw the javelin like the champion, inspired by Železný's technique and success.

As Neeraj's performances steadily improved, surpassing the 70-metre mark through relentless practice, an unexpected accident occurred in 2013. While playing basketball, Neeraj suffered a painful fall, rendering his arm immobile. Friends quickly took him to a nearby hospital, where it was discovered that his left arm was fractured. This injury abruptly halted his training, and he was sidelined for four months. During this time, he even went home to recover but never considered quitting the sport. While his arm was injured, Neeraj continued to exercise his legs, keeping his fitness levels up.

Once his arm was fully healed, he vigorously resumed his training sessions. In May 2013, the announcement of the

10th National Youth Competition came, which was to be held in the scorching heat at B.R. Stadium in Guntur, Andhra Pradesh. This competition was particularly significant as the top two winners would qualify for international events. On May 20th, the javelin throw competition commenced, featuring 14 competitors from across the country, but only three were consistently throwing over 60 metres.

By the fifth round, Neeraj was in third place. Given that only the top two performers would qualify for international competitions, Neeraj gave everything in the sixth and final round. With a throw of 65.68 metres, he managed to secure the silver medal, while his competitor from Haryana, Mandeep Kumar, clinched the gold with a throw of 67.02 metres. This achievement not only marked a significant comeback for Neeraj but also highlighted his resilience and determination to succeed despite setbacks.

Neeraj Chopra, along with Mandeep Kumar, was selected for the World Youth Athletics Championship in Ukraine, marking a significant milestone as it was Neeraj's first international tour. In the days leading up to the departure, intensive training sessions were held at the athletics field in Panchkula. Preparation involved more than just physical training; Neeraj also had to get his passport ready for his first ever flight, from Delhi to Ukraine. This was a new and thrilling experience not just for him, but for almost all the young athletes traveling with him. The pressure of competing on such a global stage was immense.

The championship took place in Donetsk, a city in the eastern part of Ukraine. As the competition commenced, the Indian team faced a series of challenging performances. On July 12, 2013, during the afternoon session, Neeraj participated in the qualification round of javelin throw. The event was fiercely competitive, featuring 36 athletes from around the world vying for medals. Lassi Särihen of Finland led the qualification in Group A with a throw of 78.75 metres, the longest in the qualifiers. Matij from Slovenia secured the second place with a throw of 76.73 metres, and Norbert from Hungary was also in the medal contention with a performance of 74 metres. Unfortunately, Mandeep Kumar from India slipped to the 15th position.

This setting provided Neeraj and his teammates a glimpse of the high standards and intense competition at the international level, offering them invaluable experience and exposure to world-class athletics.

On July 12th, the performance of the javelin throwers in Group B was less impressive compared to Group A. Oliver from Finland was the only athlete in Group B to cross 75 metres. Lassi Särihen of Finland, who had achieved 78 metres, was favoured to win the gold, setting a high benchmark.

After recovering from his arm injury, this was Neeraj's first competition. He threw a personal best of 66.75 metres in his first attempt of the season, but it was still short of the qualification mark. The top twelve athletes, who needed to throw at least 71 metres to qualify, moved on to the finals.

Neeraj's third attempt resulted in a foul, ending his participation in his first international competition. Disheartened, he left the field as the victorious athletes were being presented with their medals, highlighting the celebrations of athletes from various countries as their national anthems played and their flags were raised. The absence of the Indian flag on the victory stands struck Neeraj profoundly.

Despite the setback and a sleepless night, Neeraj did not miss attending the final round the next day to support his peers. His presence at the field, despite not qualifying for the finals, underscored his commitment and sportsmanship, observing and learning from the experiences of others as they competed at the global level.

In the final rounds of the javelin throw competition, Finland's Lassi Saarijärvi, who had topped the qualifying round, failed to secure a medal. Slovenia's Matija Muhar threw the longest distance of 78.84 metres, earning the gold and placing

Slovenia on the medals tally with this solitary gold. Hungary's Norbert Rivasz-Tóth claimed silver, while Spain's Pablo unexpectedly took bronze. When the final rankings were announced, Neeraj Chopra was placed 19th.

Disheartened, Neeraj said goodbye to Ukraine and boarded the plane back home, resolving to return only with a medal from international fields. The defeated Indian team landed at Delhi airport. While the players dispersed to their respective states, Neeraj, without going home, went straight to Panchkula. After some rest, he dedicated himself entirely to the field, striving to surpass 70 metres.

2014 dawned with the Commonwealth and Asian Games, and that year also marked the Youth Olympic Games. Neeraj, along with other under-23 Indian athletes, continued their relentless training. The 11th Youth Athletics Championships were to be held in Goa, and Neeraj was fully prepared for it.

From April 20 to 22, 2014, the 11th Youth Athletics Championships were set to unfold in Panaji, blessed with an azure coastline. The winners of this competition were to be selected for the Youth Olympics qualification in Bangkok, thus marking this event with significant importance.

The Haryana team, along with Neeraj, arrived in Panaji by train. The javelin throw competition was scheduled for the afternoon of April 22, 2014. Competitors from Delhi, Uttar Pradesh, Uttarakhand, Madhya Pradesh, Rajasthan,

Chhattisgarh, Haryana, and the host, Goa, were poised to contest for the medals.

The hard work of the past year shone brightly in Neeraj's performance. He was the only athlete from India to throw 70.02 metres, securing the gold medal. Rajesh Kumar from Uttar Pradesh, who had to settle for the silver medal, threw 67 metres. Neeraj qualified for the Bangkok competition. A total of 19 athletes, including 14 boys and 5 girls, were selected for the Youth Olympic qualification based on their performances in the Goa competition.

> **The results of the 11th National Youth Athletics Championship 2014, Goa Event:**
>
> **Event:** Javelin Throw
> **Gold Medal:** Neeraj Chopra, Haryana, 70.02 metres
> **Silver Medal:** Rajesh Kumar, Uttar Pradesh, 67.00 metres
> **Bronze Medal:** Abhishek Drall, Delhi, 66.99 metres

For the Youth Olympic qualification, the Indian team, accompanied by Coach Wazir Singh, departed from Delhi to Bangkok on May 17, 2014. Neeraj's competition was scheduled for May 22. It would be the second time he was representing India at an international competition. At 10 A.M., the qualifying round began with competitors from India, South Korea, Thailand, Malaysia, Chinese Taipei, and China. From the first round, Xiang from China took the lead with a throw of 74.59 metres, indicating he would be the likely winner. Neeraj started with a throw of 60.86 metres, coming second. In the second round, Xiang threw a gold-winning distance of 78.69 metres while Neeraj improved to 64 metres. In the third round of the first stage, Neeraj put in his best efforts and threw 70.54 metres, still 8 metres behind Xiang. Neeraj's performance in the second stage worsened, culminating in a foul on his final and sixth throw.

As expected, Xiang Jiabo from China won the gold medal and qualified for the Youth Olympics. Although Neeraj did not qualify, he wore a smile on his face, having secured his first international silver medal. Despite achieving this silver victory, he did not celebrate for long, recognizing he was still 10 metres short of winning at the international youth level. He realized he needed more effort and technique adjustments as he travelled back home from Bangkok.

Youth Olympic Qualification Event - May 2014

Event: Javelin Throw
Gold Medal: Xiang Jiabo, China, 78.69 metres
Silver Medal: Neeraj Chopra, India, 70.54 metres
Bronze Medal: Kim Woo-jang, South Korea, 66.43 metres

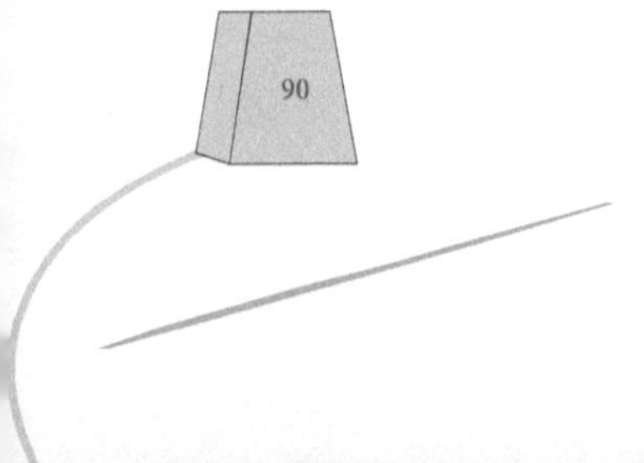

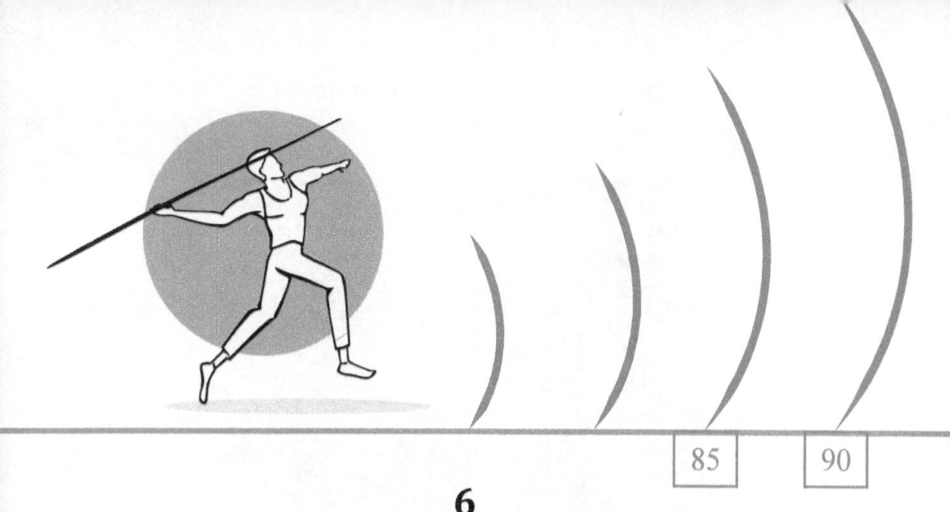

6

The Path of Defeat

Neeraj did not qualify for the 2014 Youth Olympics. Carrying the pain of this failure, he resolved to make radical changes to his javelin throw technique. In August 2014, the Asian Games were held in South Korea. He was aware that the Indian flag had not been hoisted in the javelin throw event in the premier competition of the continent. The qualifying round for the 2016 Rio Olympics was beckoning him. To prepare, young Neeraj was toiling hard on the fields of Panchkula.

For many years, no Olympic games, meaning national sports competitions, had been held in India. In February 2015, the moment was set for the national competition in Kerala. The thrill of athletics was to unfold in Trivandrum. Even though he was in the junior category, Neeraj's excellent performance secured his selection from the Haryana team for the national competition.

The torch of the 35th National Sports Competition appeared in P.T. Usha's state of Kerala in 2015. The competition was grandly inaugurated by Bharat Ratna, Sachin Tendulkar, the brand ambassador, showcasing Kerala's tradition. In the first week of the competition, Haryana's wrestlers left their mark, winning 18 out of 24 gold medals in the wrestling arena—a remarkable achievement.

Maharashtra, which had been leading due to the magic of its 34 medals in athletics, was surpassed by Kerala, which soared to second place towards the end of the competition. Haryana and Maharashtra maintained their third and fourth positions, respectively, with the armed forces team in the top spot. On the evening of February 12, 2015, competitions

in the throwing events were to unfold, involving the top 20 athletes from various states including Uttar Pradesh, West Bengal, Rajasthan, Delhi, Bihar, Uttarakhand, Kerala, Punjab, Jharkhand, and Madhya Pradesh. Out of these, 12 players were selected through the qualifying rounds, including Neeraj, who was in the junior category.

Competing in national sports competitions and winning medals is a dream cherished by every athlete in the country. The National Games in Kerala were Neeraj's first ever. However, he faced tough competition in his category. The javelin throw event started on February 12 at the athletics field in Trivandrum. A competitor from Haryana set a national record with a throw of 82.23 metres, claiming the gold medal. Neeraj's name was not on that medal. Another competitor earned the title of the new national champion with the longest throw on his second attempt. The other 11 athletes could only manage throws up to 75 metres. Haryana dominated the javelin throw, but Neeraj, another athlete from Haryana, finished in the fifth place with a throw of 73.45 metres. In his first National Games, Neeraj had to return empty-handed.

Despite his defeat at the National Games, the competition proved to be a turning point in Neeraj's career. His promising performance led to his selection for the national camp. Previously training in Panchkula, Neeraj was now set to train with the nation's top athletes at the Sports Authority of India's training centre in Patiala. The facilities in Panchkula were inadequate for throws over 80 metres, so he was ready to move to a better-equipped venue.

No one in Neeraj's family objected to his path. After finishing his 12th-grade exams, Neeraj moved to Patiala, where the Netaji Subhash National Institute of Sports awaited him. He was eager to meet new fields, fellow athletes, and coaches. Although he was defeated in the National Games, his desire to win remained strong, which was a significant factor in his selection for the camp. This dedication was set to contribute to a golden era in India's sports, with Patiala's grounds shaping many Asian, World, and Olympic athletes. In this elite group, Neeraj Chopra was poised to become a shining gem.

Neeraj quickly adapted to the competitive atmosphere at the national athletics camp in Patiala within a month. In May 2015, the 19th National Athletics Federation Cup was announced, set to take place at the Mangalam Stadium in Mangalore, Karnataka. This competition was significant as it would select the Indian team for the 21st Asian Athletics Championships in China. Athletes from across the state entered the stadium determined to secure their spot.

Neeraj travelled by train from Patiala to Mangalore. On May 2, 2015, at 5 P.M., the excitement of the javelin throw began. Although still junior, Neeraj was competing in the open category. He faced stiff competition from Haryana's Rajinder Singh, who had previously thrown beyond 82 metres but managed only 71 metres this time, slipping to fourth place. Devander Singh from the armed forces, who threw an impressive 79.65 metres, secured the gold medal. Neeraj, with a focused and determined effort, surpassed Rajinder Singh and Delhi's Rohit Kumar in the second round, achieving second place. His fourth-round throw of 73.96 metres earned him a silver medal.

Neeraj first hoisted the flag of success in the senior category at the National Athletics Federation Cup in 2015. He was more thrilled about being selected for the Asian Championships than his achievement of a silver medal. It was the first time Neeraj was being selected for the Asian Games in the senior category. The top two winners from the competition were eligible for the Asian Championships: Devander Singh from the armed forces and Neeraj Chopra from Haryana.

> **The 19th National Athletics Federation Cup 2015 results were:**
>
> **Gold Medal:** Devander Singh, Armed Forces, 79.65 metres
> **Silver Medal:** Neeraj Chopra, Haryana, 73.96 metres
> **Bronze Medal:** Rohit Kumar, Delhi, 72.72 metres

The 21st Asian Athletics Championships were scheduled from June 3 to 7 in Wuhan, China. A large team of 42 Indian athletes participated. The hosts, China, were leading in the medal tally. On June 6th, though both the discus throw and javelin throw events were anticipated, all eyes were on Vikas Gowda's discus throw. Gowda, as expected, clinched gold. Following the discus throw, the javelin competition started, featuring athletes from Chinese Taipei, Uzbekistan, Japan, Sri Lanka, China, Indonesia, Saudi Arabia, and India vying to see who could throw the farthest. However, no one managed a throw over 80 metres. Athletes from Chinese Taipei, Uzbekistan, and Japan emerged as winners with throws around 79 metres. Devander Singh and Neeraj Chopra from India performed poorly, with throws of 71.28 metres and 70.50 metres, respectively, placing them 8th and 9th.

As the medal ceremony for the discus throw was being conducted, with the Indian national anthem playing and the flag hoisting for Vikas Gowda's victory, Neeraj Chopra solemnly left the field. Standing still, he was moved by the national anthem as the stadium rose in respect. Deep in thought, Neeraj envisioned a day when the athletics field would stand in ovation for him, dreaming of the moment when he, too, would raise the national flag on the victory podium.

At the Asian Athletics Championships in China, India shone brightly, securing a total of 13 medals, including four golds, and finishing third in the medal tally. The athletes received a warm welcome upon their return, and the medallists were awarded cash prizes. Despite his defeat, Neeraj Chopra went directly to Patiala from Delhi airport, determined to exceed the 80-metre mark in his future attempts. Having passed his twelfth grade, he enrolled at DAV College in Chandigarh for his undergraduate studies.

DAV College in Sector 10, Chandigarh, is a prestigious institution under Punjab University. It has been the educational home for many international sports figures, including cricketer Kapil Dev, shooter Anjum Moudgil, hockey player Sukhbir Gill, and footballer Gurpreet Sandhu. Although Neeraj joined the arts stream, his rigourous training schedule meant that he spent more time on the field than in college. As a result, he missed out on typical college experiences like hanging out with friends, enjoying canteen tea, and participating in various college day celebrations.

While studying at DAV College, Neeraj Chopra secured a medal at the Federation Cup, marking his debut in senior international competitions. After August, the collegiate competition season began. Neeraj won at the inter-collegiate and inter-departmental levels, qualifying for the inter-university competition. The 76th All India Inter-University Championships were set to take place from December 29, 2015, to January 3, 2016, at the Punjab University grounds in Patiala.

The new year began, and on January 1, 2016, at 2:30 P.M., collegiate athletes from across India gathered for the javelin throw event. Neeraj had shown remarkable improvement since arriving in Patiala. This progress was evident on the first day of the new year when Neeraj unleashed a throw of 81.04 metres, setting a new competition record. Prior to this, no collegiate athlete in the country had managed to throw the javelin beyond 80 metres. Neeraj created history in his debut at the All-India Inter-University Championships, a record that remains unbroken to this day.

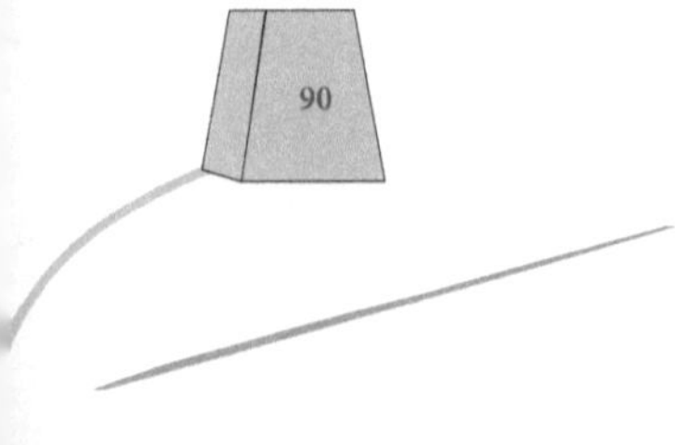

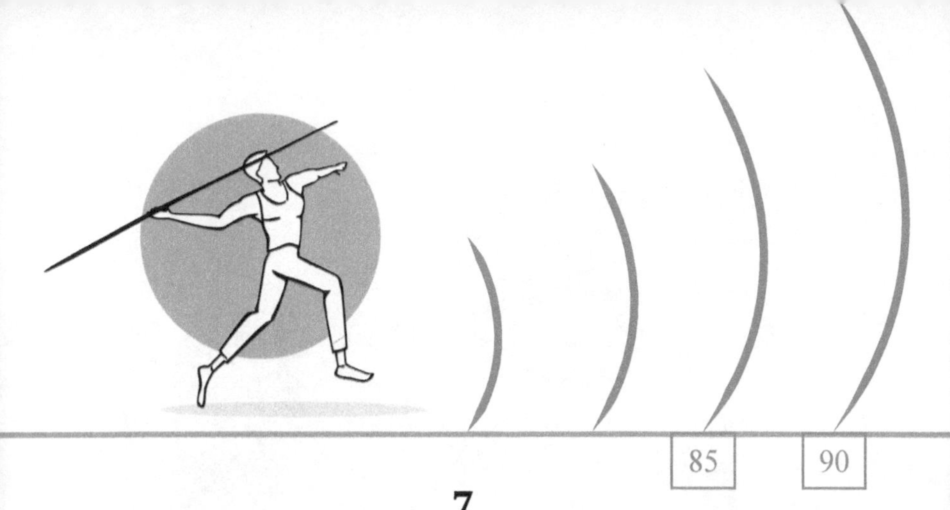

7

World Record Holder

The new Olympic year 2016 dawned. The Olympic Games were set to be celebrated in Rio de Janeiro, Brazil. The entire world was gearing up for the Olympics. With javelin throws exceeding 80 metres, Neeraj too was in sight of qualifying for the Olympics. On the very first day of the year, Neeraj had made headlines at the All India Inter-University Championships. Having set a new competition record, Neeraj was also hailed as the best athlete of the tournament.

Neeraj's development continued at the national camp in Patiala. There, Kashinath Naik, a member of the armed forces and a javelin thrower himself, was Neeraj's coach. For the first time in his life, Neeraj had a dedicated coach for javelin throw. When he joined the camp in Patiala in 2015, he was the youngest athlete there. Even as a junior, his performance

surpassed many senior athletes, leading to his selection for the Indian team for the 2016 South Asian Games. Neeraj, along with Samarjeet Singh, was set to represent India in javelin throw.

The 12th South Asian Games took place from February 5 to 16, 2016, in Guwahati, the capital of Assam. The games were inaugurated by India's sports-loving Prime Minister, Shri Narendra Modi, with great fanfare. As expected, India began winning gold medals from the first day of the competition. The javelin throw event was scheduled to start at 4 P.M. on February 10.

The South Asian Games are organized every four years, following the model of the Olympics. Eight countries from the South Asian region participate: Sri Lanka, Bhutan, Maldives,

Bangladesh, Pakistan, Nepal, Afghanistan, and India. In the javelin throw competition, a fierce rivalry was expected between India, Sri Lanka, and Pakistan. India's Neeraj Chopra, Sri Lanka's D.S. Ransinghe, and Pakistan's Arshad Nadeem were all capable of throwing around 80 metres. One of these three was poised to clinch the gold medal.

Athletes from India, Pakistan, Sri Lanka, as well as Nepal and Bangladesh, were ready to compete. Neeraj's performance at the Indira Gandhi Stadium in Guwahati mirrored his Olympic gameplay in Tokyo. He declared his supremacy on the field right from the first round with a throw of 82.23 metres, claiming that he was the champion of this arena. Sri Lanka's Ransinghe reached 80.25 metres on his fifth attempt, while Pakistan's Nadeem managed a throw of 78.33 metres.

India, Sri Lanka, and Pakistan respectively won gold, silver, and bronze medals. Neeraj, with his outstanding performance, set a new competition record, surpassing the previous mark of 78.01 metres set by India's Jagdish Bishnoi in 1999. Neeraj's performance at the All India Inter-University and the SAFF Games had made him a notable athlete. He was just 1 metre short of the Olympic qualifying standard. With the Olympics beckoning him, he was training intensely on the field.

The SAFF Games had also ignited a traditional rivalry in javelin throw between India and Pakistan. The competition between Neeraj Chopra and Pakistan's Arshad Nadeem was expected to extend to the Asian and Olympic Games. Neeraj's journey to keep the Indian flag flying high had begun. Given that it was an Olympic year, foreign coaches were invited to India for various sports. For javelin, Australia's Garry Calvert was brought to Patiala, and his arrival marked significant changes in Neeraj's technique. Garry Calvert, who had been the chief coach of the Chinese national team, served as the special coach for Indian javelin throwers from February 2016 to April 2017. From day one, the calm Neeraj and Garry Calvert resonated well with each other, with Calvert almost becoming a godfather to Neeraj.

Unaffected by the heat, wind, or rain, Neeraj's athletic dedication continued. He was deeply immersed in the modern training methods of his new coach, Garry Calvert, striving to qualify for the Olympics. The Indian Athletics Federation decided to organize the Indian Grand Prix in three stages to provide Indian athletes with the opportunity to meet Olympic qualifying standards on home soil. The first stage took place on Sunday, April 24, 2016, at the Jawaharlal Nehru Stadium in Delhi, where Neeraj participated. In this competition, Neeraj led in performance throughout and reached a distance of 79.54 metres in his final attempt of six throws. However, he could not meet the Olympic standard of 83 metres. During these intense efforts to achieve his best throw, he suffered a severe strain in his back. The impact was so forceful that it resulted in an injury.

In April 2016, Neeraj was scheduled to participate in the 14th Federation Cup at the Kanteerava Stadium in Bangalore.

However, he was troubled by a back injury. The injury worsened, forcing him to withdraw from the competition. It was the first time in his career that he was side-lined by an injury. Consequently, for the first time in his life, although his participation was confirmed, he was unable to compete.

Neeraj had just four months left to qualify for the Olympics. Due to his injury, he could not compete in the second stage of the Indian Grand Prix held in Patiala. Other javelin throwers also failed to meet the Olympic qualifying standards. His training came to a complete halt due to the injury, making it impossible for him to compete. The final date for Olympic qualification was July 11, 2016. Neeraj's back injury prevented him from competing, and as a result, he missed his first chance to participate in the Rio Olympics.

As his injury was not very serious, Neeraj was able to return to the field within two months after taking adequate rest. During this challenging period, Gary Calvert stood by him as his sole companion. Many thought Neeraj would never play again, but Calvert facilitated his recovery through proper physiotherapy. They resumed training with exercises that didn't put excessive strain on his back. Neeraj spent more time in the gym to regain strength and durability, with the medicine ball becoming a close ally. Post-training, Coach Calvert emphasized exercises essential for cooling the body to ensure Neeraj's full recovery and taught him how to prevent future injuries.

Injuries can abruptly halt the careers of talented athletes. Without timely and appropriate treatment, a flourishing sports career can come to a permanent stop. Excessive training without supplementary exercises often leads to injuries. Olympic bronze medallist in tennis, Leander Paes, and cricket legend, Sachin Tendulkar, both suffered from tennis elbow for a long time. Through proper treatment, both were able to make successful comebacks and triumph in their respective fields.

After overcoming his injury, Neeraj made a comeback and was selected for the Asian Junior Athletics Championships. In June 2016, he travelled to Vietnam with Coach Calvert for the 17th Asian Junior Athletics Championships.

This was Neeraj's last chance to qualify for the Olympics. The competition in Vietnam, held from June 3 to 6, 2016, featured 44 sports events. Athletes born between 1997 and 2000 from 45 countries were going to showcase their skills in this junior competition.

On June 6, 2016, during the afternoon session, events like the 400 metres hurdles, triple jump, 800 metres race, and javelin throw were all set to start simultaneously. Japan's Haruko won the 400 metres hurdles. The spotlight continued to shine on Japan in the javelin throw as well. The javelin throw event ignited fierce competition among participants from Japan, India, Uzbekistan, China, Iraq, South Korea, Chinese Taipei, Kazakhstan, and Pakistan.

The competition for medals was intense between Japan, India, and Pakistan. Neeraj, recently recovered from his injury, threw the javelin 77.60 metres, securing a position favourable for winning a medal. However, Japan's Sado Juni edged out Neeraj by only 0.37 metres, throwing 77.97 metres to snatch the gold medal. The bronze medal was claimed by Pakistan's Nadeem Arshad. None of the competitors was able to achieve the Olympic qualifying mark of 83 metres.

At the Asian Junior Athletics Championships in Vietnam, Japan's Sado Junya not only won the gold but also set a new competition record with his throw of 77.97 metres. Neeraj Chopra from India, who was the true contender for the gold, managed a throw of 77.60 metres. Limited by his recent

recovery and reduced training, he could not reach beyond 77 metres. Neeraj was more disappointed about missing the chance at the Olympics than missing the gold medal. Despite having the capability to throw over 83 metres, the injury had set him back, a fact that Coach Garry Calvert was also acutely aware of.

With the support of his foreign coach, Neeraj won his first international silver medal, marking his successful international comeback. Even though he missed the chance to compete in the Olympics, Coach Garry Calvert and the spirited Neeraj Chopra focused all their efforts on the World Junior Athletics Championships. Missing the 2016 Olympics deprived Neeraj of a golden opportunity for yet another unprecedented success at the games. For this, Coach Garry Calvert and Neeraj worked tirelessly, setting their sights beyond the Olympic qualifying standard of 83 metres.

Just days before the Olympics began, the announcement for the World Junior Athletics Championships came. Neeraj continued his rigorous training sessions in preparation for this global junior event to be held in Poland.

At the Sports Authority of India's athletics training centre in Bangalore, Neeraj and Coach Calvert were engaged in intensive training sessions both morning and evening. Under the skilled technical guidance of Coach Calvert, Neeraj's javelin throw technique underwent significant improvement, enabling him to throw the javelin further and with greater precision. On the training grounds of Bangalore, Neeraj's javelin consistently surpassed the Olympic qualifying mark of 83 metres, reaching distances up to 87 metres—a feat no other Indian athlete had achieved before. Had it not been for his injury, Neeraj would have easily qualified for the Rio Olympics. The final date for Olympic qualification was July 11.

Following this event, the World Junior Athletics Championships for athletes under 20 were set to take place in Poland from July 19th. Neeraj, a nineteen-year-old first-year college student, was preparing rigorously for this global junior event. His potential to achieve unprecedented success was apparent, though only Coach Calvert was truly confident that this young Indian could conquer the world stage.

From Delhi, a team of 27 athletes departed for the World Junior Athletics Championships. The event was set to take place from July 19 to 24 in Bydgoszcz, Poland, known as the cultural capital of the country. This global gathering of athletes under twenty years old was to feature participants from 140 countries worldwide. In 44 sporting events, 1,359 athletes were to vie for medals. The excitement of this biennial world championship was to unfold on the blue synthetic track of the Zdzisław Krzyszkowiak Stadium. No Indian had ever won a gold medal at this event, so expectations for the 27 Indian athletes were modest, primarily anticipated to participate without contending for top honours against powerhouses like the USA, Kenya, Russia, China, and Germany. After his injury, there were no expectations from Neeraj to win a medal either.

The International Association of Athletics Federations (IAAF) had renamed the competition to the IAAF World U20 Championships, underlining its significance as a premier event for young athletes globally.

The event was originally scheduled to be held on January 7, 2016, in Russia. However, due to the suspension of the Russian Athletics Federation, the championships were postponed. Ultimately, the city of Bydgoszcz in Poland stepped up to host the event, which took place six months later than planned. Perhaps it was fate that delayed the event, possibly giving the Indian flag a chance to be hoisted highest.

From the first day of the competition on July 19, 2016, similar to the Olympics, the tales of India's defeats began on the athletics track of the global youth championships. Indian athletes struggled to make an impact in the finals. In events like long jump and shot put, India's performance was lacklustre.

The morning of July 22, 2016, brought a ray of hope for India. A nineteen-year-old young athlete was waving the Indian flag high from his very first throw in the javelin event. It was his first world competition, and naturally, he felt immense pressure. There was the intimidating performance of foreign athletes, and his teammates had faced defeats, yet he did not retreat. Carrying the disappointment of missing the Olympic qualification, he entered the field determined to excel. Dressed in a black tracksuit and a blue jersey, Neeraj stepped onto the field aiming for his best performance.

On the morning of July 22, 2016, the qualification round took place, deciding who among the world's top young athletes from 33 countries and 36 javelin throwers would stand out. Neeraj was set to prove his qualification in Group A. His group included competitors like Anderson Peters from the small Caribbean nation of Grenada, Arshad Nadeem, a traditional rival from Pakistan, and athletes from powerhouse nations like the USA, Poland, Ukraine, Russia, South Africa, Japan, South Korea, Brazil, China, England, and France.

July 22, 2016, marked a promising morning for India in the World Junior Athletics Championships. The javelin throw competition commenced with the qualification round setting a mark of 72.50 metres to determine the top 12 athletes. Wearing jersey number 458, Neeraj was scheduled to throw second among 18 competitors. Leading into the 2016 season, Neeraj's name was highlighted as having the best performance, with no other competitor having thrown beyond 80 metres. On paper, Neeraj was the top contender.

The reality on the field swiftly confirmed this. The first to throw, Brazil's Pedro Barros, managed a best effort of just around 67 metres in three attempts. When Neeraj's turn came, he immediately made a statement. With his very first throw, he launched the javelin to 78.20 metres, the best among all 36 participants, unequivocally claiming his dominance of the field. This performance not only led the qualifying round but also set him apart by nearly 2 metres from other qualifiers like athletes from Poland, Ukraine, and England.

Neeraj's throw reflected the adage, "We never stand behind anyone; where we stand, the line starts from there." He showcased an Olympic-level miracle four years early in the qualification round of this global youth event, proving his mettle and setting high expectations for his future performances.

Reaching the finals of the World Junior Championships, Neeraj reignited hopes for a medal for India, a nation that had never before seen a gold in the under-20 World Junior Athletics Championships. This new feat was within reach, and Neeraj's journey there had begun in earnest. Coach Calvert was the first to congratulate him, providing guidance to keep his mind calm. He knew that the battle was only halfway won, and many athletes leading in the qualification rounds often faced defeats in the finals. Calvert focused on boosting Neeraj's mental resilience as well as his physical fitness.

The final showdown was set for the afternoon session the next day, July 22, 2016, stretching into the morning of July 23. Calvert spent the entire day and the following morning until 5 A.M. boosting Neeraj's confidence, visualizing consistent and powerful throws. Neeraj spent the night mentally replaying the finals, and after ample rest, engaged in preparatory exercises in the morning. His standout performance in the qualifiers, throwing 2 metres further than anyone else, had significantly eased his nerves while simultaneously increasing the pressure on the other 13 finalists. Neeraj was ready to hoist the Indian flag at the highest spot in the World Junior Championships for the first time.

Sporting a military-style haircut, Neeraj donned a black tracksuit with white stripes and a half jersey emblazoned with 'INDIA'. With a confident expression, he stepped onto the blue synthetic track of the Zdzisław Krzyszkowiak Stadium in Bydgoszcz. On the fifth consecutive day of the World Junior Championships, there were just a few spectators at the stadium for the finals of eight sports. Among them, Neeraj was the lone representative from India in the finals on that day, as no other Indian athlete had qualified for the final events. With a population of over a billion, all of India's hopes rested solely on Neeraj.

As the sun set on July 23rd, the competition to determine the world's best junior javelin thrower intensified in the first round. The battlefield of javelin throw included athletes from 14 countries. India made its mark right from the first round, with Neeraj throwing an encouraging 79.66 metres, leading the initial throws. Anderson Peters from Grenada, also a strong contender, was not far behind, making his presence felt with a throw of 79.51 metres in his first attempt.

However, Johan Grobler from South Africa, who was initially in fourth place, surpassed them both on his subsequent attempt, throwing an impressive 80.59 metres, setting the best mark of the competition till then. The crowd in the stadium, filled with excitement, waved the South African flags high as Grobler took the lead. This performance not only highlighted the fierce competition but also set a high standard for the remaining rounds, putting pressure on Neeraj and the other leading competitors to surpass this new benchmark.

Now, the competition for medals was clearly between South Africa, Grenada, and India. Challengers from Hungary, Ukraine, England, Poland, France, Japan, Bulgaria, and Turkistan had been effectively outperformed. For the first time in many years, India's tricolour was poised to wave high at a global athletics event, and this time, potentially even higher than before. Previously, Seema Antil in 2002 and Navjeet Kaur in 2014 had each earned a bronze medal in discus throw, marking significant achievements. Neeraj, however, was poised to surpass this historical benchmark as the first Indian to potentially go beyond a bronze in javelin throw at the World Junior Championships. The anticipation for the second round of javelin throws was palpable, with no one able to predict the level of performance that was about to unfold.

After the first round was completed, featuring competitors from 14 countries including the athlete from the small nation of Latvia, the second round quickly commenced. The commentary for Neeraj Chopra from India started ramping up on the sports channel. Concurrently, the 10,000 metres race was unfolding on the track, adding to the bustling atmosphere of the stadium.

Holding a javelin coloured in a mix of blue, yellow, and green, Neeraj took a confident run-up. As he crossed more than half the distance of the runway, he drew the javelin back, channelling all his energy into the throw. With precise direction, he launched it into the air. As the javelin soared, Neeraj's hands touched the ground to stabilize his throw, ensuring a perfect landing. He then turned to watch the javelin's flight, raising his right hand to acknowledge the crowd as the javelin, like a bullet from a gun, continued its trajectory through the air. Moments later, it landed well beyond the marked line on the lush green field.

The commentator exclaimed in astonishment, "Oh my goodness!" A new world record was set at 86.48 metres, a performance beyond historical comparisons, unexpectedly achieved by Neeraj. The other competitors rushed to congratulate him, acknowledging this phenomenal achievement that placed him firmly at the pinnacle of the junior world stage.

Neeraj Chopra's performance in the open category at the World Junior Championships was nothing short of spectacular. He achieved a throw that was 3 metres beyond the Olympic

qualifying mark, a feat that could have seen him competing at the Olympics, if only the timing had aligned. Unfortunately, due to the scheduling delays, the World Championships in Poland occurred just a little too late, causing Neeraj to miss his chance at the Rio Olympics, along with an opportunity for an Olympic medal for his country.

In his debut at the World Junior Championships, Neeraj not only competed but also set a new world record in javelin throw. The previous record held by Zigismunds Sirmais of Latvia was 84.69 metres, and Neeraj shattered this with a throw of 86.48 metres, exceeding it by nearly 2 metres. This record-setting performance established Neeraj as a prominent figure on the global athletics stage and his world record in the junior championships remains unbroken to this day, showcasing his extraordinary talent and the bright future that lay ahead of him in the sport.

During the World Junior Championships, the javelin throw competition unfolded over four rounds. In the third round, Neeraj Chopra managed a throw of 78.36 metres, but he fouled in the fourth round. However, it was his throw in the second round that became historic. With a world record-breaking throw, he became the first Indian athlete to win a gold medal at the World Junior Championships. Johan Grobler from South Africa, who led after the first round, faltered from the second round onwards and settled for silver with his best throw in the final round. Anderson Peters from Grenada, inspired by Neeraj, threw 79.65 metres in the second round to secure the bronze medal.

Neeraj's performance significantly outpaced all other competitors. The difference between his throw and the performances of other athletes was as much as 6 metres, showcasing his dominance. His record-setting effort not only established a new world junior record but also surpassed the existing national record, marking a monumental achievement that resonated well beyond the national borders.

The entire world was in awe of Neeraj's performance. For the first time in the history of World Junior Athletics, the Indian tricolour soared highest on the victory podium. Neeraj accepted his gold medal amidst the historic setting of his world record performance. The national anthem of India, "Jana Gana Mana," resonated through the stadium, marking a profound moment as it played at the World Junior Championships for the first time ever.

Meanwhile, at the Rio Olympics, Thomas from Germany clinched the gold medal with a spectacular throw of 90 metres. Keshorn Walcott from Trinidad and Tobago secured the bronze with a throw of 85.38 metres. Had Neeraj qualified for the Rio Olympics, his performances suggested that he could have been a contender for the medal as well. However, fate had different plans for him. Neeraj was not just to be an Olympic medallist, but he was being shaped to become an Olympic champion.

The stage was being set for him at the upcoming Tokyo Olympics. Before that, he was to leave his mark at the Asian Games and the Commonwealth Games, aiming to consistently hoist the Indian flag at the highest ranks. The journey ahead was clear—Neeraj was determined to keep the tricolour waving proudly on the global stage.

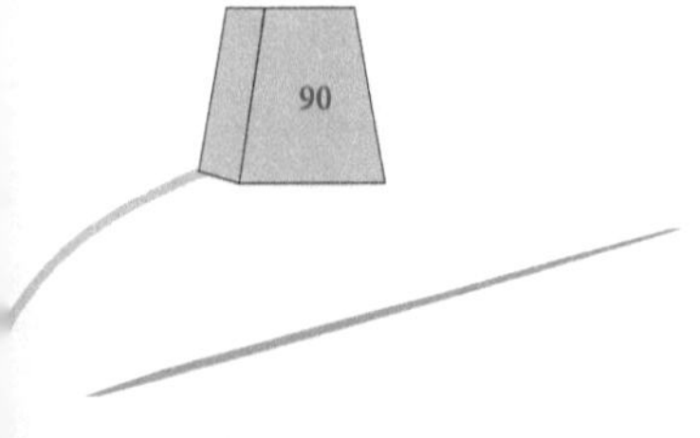

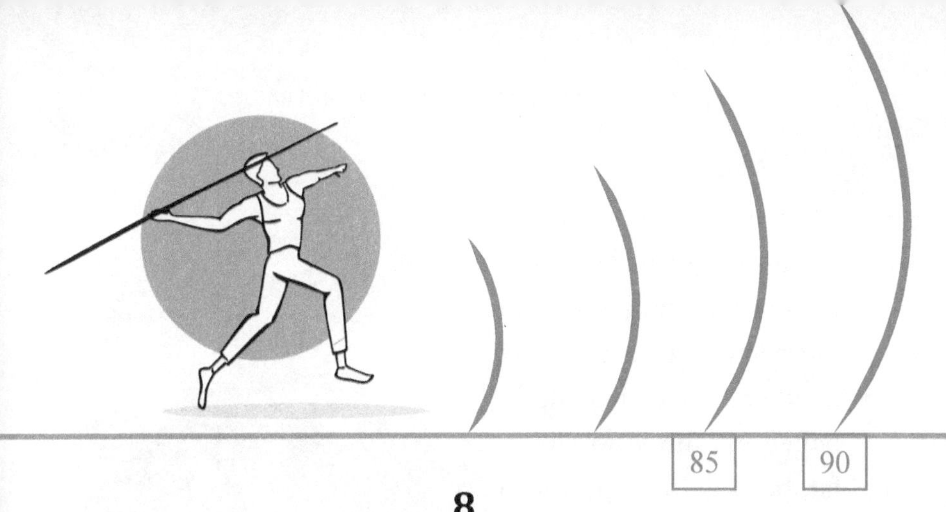

8

Victory Cry of the Army Man

Neeraj Chopra's world-record performance had brought unprecedented glory to the Indian tricolour in the global athletics arena. As the national flag was hoisted in the highest place of honour, a digital screen displaying his monumental throw of 86.48 metres alongside his image became a focal point for photographers from all over the world. The scene was bustling as they gathered to capture this historic moment.

Although only a select few Indians, including Coach Gary Calvert, were present to witness this magnificent event, Neeraj's acclaim was universal. His remarkable achievement was celebrated worldwide, highlighting his ascent as a global athletics sensation. This milestone was not just a personal triumph for Neeraj but a monumental victory for India, positioning him as a hero who elevated the prestige of his nation on the world stage.

After becoming the world champion, journalists from around the world rushed to interview Neeraj. Speaking to them, Neeraj said, "I hoped my throw would go far, but I didn't expect it to cross 86 metres or to set a world record. My goal this year was to qualify for the Olympics. Failing to achieve that, winning a medal in the Under-20 World Championship became my ambitious target.

"My first throw was promising. When I took the javelin for the second round, I felt this throw would be special. Unexpectedly, it was better than 86 metres—a result of rigorous training over the last two months. I perfected my throwing technique and worked hard on my fitness, which transformed into a world record."

Upon his return to India, Neeraj Chopra was welcomed with grand celebrations. The Sports Authority of India

(SAI) organized a special felicitation ceremony for him in Panchkula. In his hometown of Khandra, the atmosphere was as festive as Diwali. The village panchayat honoured him, and the celebrations were joyful and vibrant. However, not lingering long in the festivities, Neeraj returned to Patiala to resume his training sessions.

During this period, he received more joyful news. The Indian Army offered him a direct position in recognition of his achievements, particularly after setting a national record at the South Asian Games. His former coach, Kashinath Naik, who had once suggested that Neeraj join the army, would have been proud to see his recommendation come to fruition.

Neeraj Chopra's family initially resisted the idea of him joining the army, as no one from their family had served in the military before. The prevailing sentiment was to allow Neeraj to play any sport he liked, except to join the army. However, the perspective began to shift following a visit by Brigadier Atish Yadav and Subedar Sunil from the Rajputana Rifles, who went to Neeraj's home in Khandra village. The army officers were warmly welcomed and enjoyed the hospitality offered by Neeraj's family.

Brigadier Yadav explained how Neeraj could be recruited into the army under the sports quota, detailing the process and benefits. Initially, Neeraj's parents were against the idea, but after discussions with the elders in the family the next day, they collectively agreed to let Neeraj join the army as an athlete. His mother also welcomed the decision, recognizing the honour and opportunities it could bring to Neeraj.

In July 2012, Neeraj Chopra's parents were delighted when he secured a job at the age of nineteen due to his capabilities as an athlete. Nine years earlier, they had been concerned about the future of Neeraj, who was then overweight. His life was transformed by the sport of javelin throw, which not only reshaped his physique but also provided him with a career opportunity, particularly in the army.

Following his success in international competitions, Neeraj accepted a position in the Indian Army. He was appointed as a Naib Subedar in the Rajputana Rifles, a rank usually not directly offered to sportsmen as they did not normally start as Junior Commissioned Officers. However, Neeraj's exceptional qualities and achievements earned him the prestigious position of Naib Subedar.

Neeraj Chopra's family had a strong military tradition. His ancestors, originally from Maharashtra, were those who fought in the Battle of Panipat and were called "Road Marathas." The history of the valiant Marathas who fought at the battlefield of Panipat is well-known. The Chopra family descends from these Marathas.

The Battle of Panipat, a significant upheaval in the history of the Marathas and of India as well, took place on January

14, 1761. Under the leadership of Peshwa Sadashivrao, the Marathas fought against Ahmad Shah Abdali and were defeated. About 50,000 Maratha soldiers were martyred in this battle. Some of the surviving soldiers took refuge right there in the vicinity of Panipat. They lived in the area known as Road, and to identify themselves, they used the term "Road Maratha," a name they still use to describe themselves today. They are a majority in about two hundred and fifty villages in the districts of Panipat, Karnal, Kurukshetra, Sonipat, Kaithal, and Rohtak. Their ancestors were adept in swordsmanship and javelin throwing, a skill that ran in Neeraj's blood. By joining the Indian Army, Neeraj had maintained his connection with both javelin throwing and his military heritage.

While the primary function of the Indian Armed Forces is to safeguard the nation, their contributions to the field of sports are also remarkable. Figures like Milkha Singh emerged as global athletes, thanks to the armed forces. The military has given the country numerous international sports figures. Olympic medallist shooters like Rajyavardhan Rathore and Vijay Kumar, who won silver at the London Olympics, were polished under the military sports schemes. Across the nation, sports training centres run by the armed forces have developed. Since the pre-independence era, the armed forces have been dedicatedly fostering global athletes. Even during the British Army times, sports were valued. In India's first Olympic hockey victory, the team had significant contributions from military personnel. Hockey legend

Dhyan Chand also rose to fame from within the ranks of the military.

Rajyavardhan Rathore, who delivered India's first individual Olympic silver medal, was a gem from the Armed Forces. His skills in shooting were honed in the military, and within just six years, he achieved Olympic glory. After fulfilling the minimum service requirement in the military, he successfully transitioned to a political career, serving as the Minister of Sports in the BJP government.

The Armed Forces provides a significant opportunity for those interested in a sports career. From as young as ten years old, children with an interest in sports can join the sports training centres of the Armed Forces. This not only allows them to serve the nation but also to excel in sports. Importantly, athletes in the military are considered national assets, hence they are not deployed in combat roles. They are expected to raise the nation's glory on the sports field, ensuring the national flag flies high.

India has numerous military units, and their annual competitions are managed by the Services Sports Control Board (SSCB). Medallists from these competitions receive specialized training to prepare them for national and international levels. SSCB is a joint organization of all three branches of the military and plays a significant role in developing athletes who raise the national flag high in sports arenas.

Each sport in India has a national federation, to which all state associations are affiliated. The military holds a special place in all these national federations and the Indian Olympic Association. The military sports teams are granted the status of a state sports organization, enabling matchups between military and state teams in national competitions. Like the Olympics, national sports competitions include military participation. Over the past decade, the military has secured the highest number of medals in the National Games, claiming the title of the best national team. Military athletes are increasingly visible in the Olympics, Asian Games, and Commonwealth Games.

Once an athlete joins the military, the stress of training costs and employment is alleviated. Winning medals often leads to immediate promotions. A simple soldier can rise to higher ranks such as Subedar or Lieutenant through exceptional performance in sports. The military is considered a gateway to discipline and patriotism, for those looking to pursue a career in sports.

For the Mission Olympic program, the military established the Army Sports Institute (ASI) in Pune in 2001. ASI aims to develop world-class athletes, maintaining a successful track record. It offers high-level training in seven sports: archery, athletics, boxing, diving, fencing, weightlifting, and wrestling. The athletes at ASI, nurtured under strict military discipline, are consistently seen exerting immense effort in their training.

The Army Sports Institute (ASI) has everything needed to develop successful athletes on a global scale. It equips athletes thoroughly through foreign coaches, sports physiologists, sports psychologists, biomechanics, sports analysts, and sports nutritionists. Athletes from ASI have won 702 international medals for the country, including participation at the Olympic level.

Enrolment at ASI begins from the age of ten. The Boys Sports Company selects youths with special aptitude in sports for advanced training at ASI. Each year, the Boys Sports Company selects 210 athletes, starting their sports training from a young age.

After the military, the Indian Railways offers direct employment to athletes. In the states of Delhi, Haryana, and Uttar Pradesh, national medal-winning athletes are directly recruited into the police force as officers. Employment provides stability to the performance of these athletes. The military secured Neeraj's future by providing him a job.

The military directly selects young athletes who have won medals at national and international levels. Following this model, Neeraj was selected for the Rajputana Rifles unit under the Mission Olympic scheme. The headquarters of the Rajputana Rifles is located in Delhi, while the headquarters and main training centre of the Army Sports Institute (ASI) are in Pune. However, Neeraj was not restricted to being stationed only at these locations; he continued his training at the Sports Authority of India's facility in Patiala, preparing for new challenges.

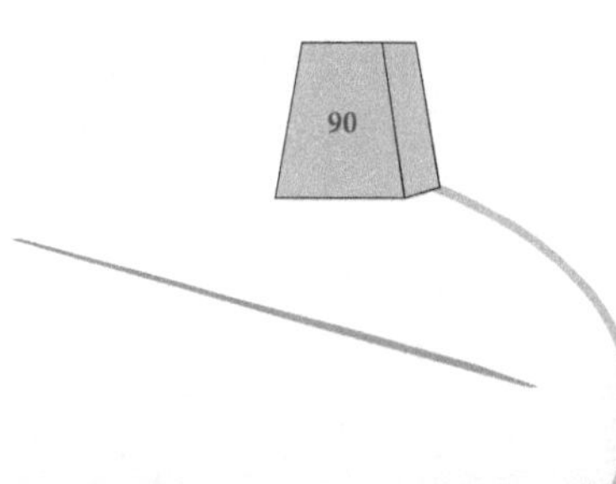

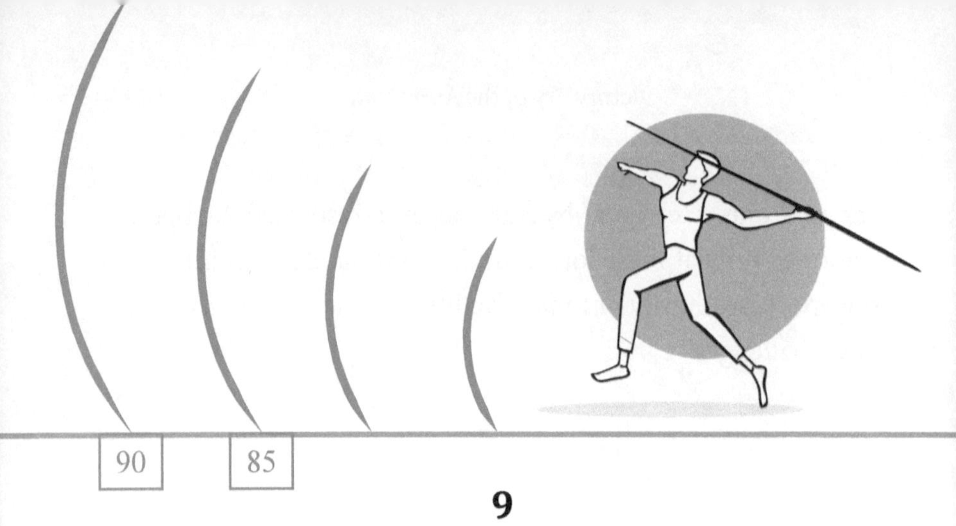

9

The Asian Record Holder

Neeraj Chopra too felt the disappointment that no Indian male athlete could secure a medal at the Rio 2016 Olympics. Had he qualified, perhaps he might have added a medal to the tally of Indian male athletes. At the Rio Olympics, Sakshi Malik clinched a bronze in wrestling and P.V. Sindhu won a silver in badminton, but the narratives of defeats were written for the other athletes.

Though Neeraj missed the Olympics, his world record-breaking performance at the World Junior Championships brought a golden glow to his career. He became the Junior World Champion in 2016. After bidding farewell to a memorable 2016, the start of the new season in 2017 promised a strong performance from Neeraj.

Neeraj Chopra's 2017 season began with a silver triumph in the Asian Grand Prix series. In April 2017, he competed in three events—two in China and one in Chinese Taipei—where he kept the Indian flag flying high. However, he did not achieve the coveted gold. In the first leg of the series on April 24 in China, he threw 82.11 metres, securing second place. Chao-Tsun Cheng of Chinese Taipei outperformed him with a throw of 84.72 metres, the best in that event, pushing Neeraj to second place. As a Junior World Champion, Neeraj was unable to match his renowned capabilities in this competition.

Just three days later, the second leg of the series was held in Jiaxing, China. Again, Neeraj did not reach the top spot in this second stage of the Asian Grand Prix. Once more, Chao-Tsun Cheng bested him by throwing an impressive 86.92 metres, clinching the gold. Neeraj managed a throw of 83.32 metres, securing his second consecutive silver medal in the series.

In the third leg of the series in Chinese Taipei, Neeraj Chopra was unable to cross even the 80-metre mark. Chao-Tsun Cheng from Taipei also fell behind in this stage. Shi Feng Huang from Taipei threw a personal best of 80.77 metres, securing first place. Chao-Tsun Cheng managed a throw of 79.93 metres, earning the silver medal. Neeraj was just 0.03 metres behind Cheng, with a throw of 79.90 metres, thus missing the chance to achieve a silver medal hat trick in the Asian Grand Prix series and had to settle for the bronze medal.

Despite setbacks in clinching gold in the Asian Grand Prix series, Neeraj's international experience continued to refine his skills. Although he did not perform his best, he maintained India's competitiveness in the events. Neeraj continued to elevate the Indian flag on the victory stand in javelin throw competitions.

In the national competitions during the 2017 season, Neeraj Chopra maintained his dominance. Foreign Coach Gary Calvert had played a significant role in mentoring and shaping Neeraj's performance during the Olympic year of 2016. In May 2017, Calvert's contract with Indian athletes ended, and he returned to his home country. In 2017, Neeraj continued intense training sessions with an Indian coach. Many athletes, including Neeraj, felt the absence of foreign coaches.

The 21st Federation Cup National Athletics Championships took place in the first week of June on the tracks of Patiala, Punjab. On June 4th, Neeraj excelled again. He took the lead right from his first throw, recording an impressive 85.63 metres, surpassing athletes from Kerala, Uttar Pradesh, Punjab, Rajasthan, West Bengal, and Haryana. The face of his former Coach Calvert lit up with joy. Within a month, the bugle for the Asian Athletics Championships was to sound, and Neeraj's performance at the Federation event acted as a booster. Proving himself as the best javelin thrower in the country, Neeraj was gearing up to establish himself as the top javelin thrower in Asia. Meanwhile, his Coach Calvert received an extension of 6 months as a special consideration.

The 22ⁿᵈ Asian Athletics Championships heralded its commencement in Bhubaneswar, the capital of Odisha, India. The event was scheduled from 6ᵗʰ to 9ᵗʰ July 2017 at the Kalinga Stadium, featuring 560 athletes from 41 countries, ready to compete in thrilling athletic events. After intensive training in Bangalore, Neeraj Chopra arrived in Bhubaneswar. From the very first day, Indian athletes started off strongly in men's running events, claiming golds. In field events like long jump, high jump, shot put, and discus throw, athletes from China, South Korea, and Iran delivered outstanding performances. The climax of the competition awaited on the final day's afternoon session, to decide who the best javelin thrower in Asia was.

The presence of gold medallists from the Asian Grand Prix series, including competitors from Chinese Taipei, heightened the unpredictability of who would clinch the javelin throw gold. With competitors like Ahmed Magour from Qatar and Pakistan's traditional rival, Arshad Nadeem, also in the fray, bets were on who would triumph. The competition saw top athletes from India, China, Chinese Taipei, Pakistan, Qatar, Uzbekistan, Hong Kong, Saudi Arabia, Bangladesh, South Korea, Sri Lanka, and Kazakhstan among the top 18 contenders in the javelin throw event.

The anticipation to see Neeraj Chopra, a world junior champion, compete had reached its peak among the spectators in Odisha. Neeraj, in top form, made his first throw but it ended in a foul, leading to profound disappointment among his fans. In the first round, Cheng Chao from Chinese Taipei led with a throw of 78.76 metres. Ahmed Magour from Qatar stayed in the medal contention from the first round. In the second round, Ahmad reached 81.53 metres, solidifying his path towards a medal. Neeraj was pushed to the fifth position in his second attempt. In the third round, Neeraj fell back further to the sixth position. He barely managed to maintain his place in the top eight for the second phase of the competition. Coach Calvert advised Neeraj "not to rush and play calmly."

With the completion of the first and crucial phase of the competition, those who threw the javelin over 81 metres were considered potential winners. A fierce battle for medals was expected among Ahmed Magour from Qatar, Davinder Singh from India, and Shih Feng Huang from Chinese Taipei. Neeraj, initially disappointed, maintained his morale. In his fourth attempt, he made a comeback with a throw of 83.06 metres, which changed the dynamics of the race for the medal. The countries now leading in the top three were Qatar, India, and India. In the fifth round, Neeraj fell back again, but the rankings did not change. Ahmed Magour, Davinder Singh, and Neeraj remained the top contenders.

The decisive sixth round began. Taking a deep breath and exhaling, Neeraj sprinted down the track for his final attempt. With a perfect landing before releasing the javelin with all his strength, a miracle happened. The javelin struck the ground at

85.23 metres, setting a new competition record. Neeraj, who was contending for a bronze, vaulted to gold. This last throw was a sight for the sore eyes of the athletics fans in Orissa, turning Neeraj into a beacon of hope from the tides of defeat. It was akin to hitting a six on the last ball to win a cricket match, demonstrating how athletics competitions could also turn in the final moments. Neeraj's explosive performance in the Asian Games had avenged his loss in the Asian Grand Prix. Shih Feng and Chao Cheng from Chinese Taipei had to return home empty-handed.

On the victory podium, flags of India and Qatar were hoisted. The Indian national anthem resonated. As chants of "Jai Hind" echoed on the track, Neeraj's performance in the field events also heralded India's triumph. With a total of 10 golds, 6 silvers, and 13 bronzes, India topped the medal tally with 29 medals. Before the Asian Games in Jakarta that year, the Commonwealth Games were set to unfold. The dominance of Indian athletics hinted at, in the Orissa competition, was expected to continue in these prestigious contests. Neeraj, who had maintained his morale until the final round, realized that with an unwavering focus and spirit, one could achieve peak performance. Now, the upcoming World Championships in London on August 24th beckoned him. Before that, he was also aiming to make his mark in the World Diamond League series. Even before the triumph in Bhubaneswar, Neeraj's career had embraced the global stage with his

participation in the Diamond League, representing India thrice during the 2017 season.

After the Asian Grand Prix, Neeraj Chopra competed in the Diamond League in Paris on July 1, 2017. It was his first Diamond League event, featuring renowned athletes. Yet Neeraj was undaunted. Competing for the first time against world champions like Johannes Vetter from Germany, Jakub Vadlejch and Vitezslav Veselý from the Czech Republic, and Thomas Röhler from Germany, Neeraj was the youngest javelin thrower at twenty years of age, among the top 10 global competitors.

In his Diamond League debut, Neeraj made a mark by throwing 84.67 metres, surpassing athletes from host nation

France, Australia, Czech Republic, Moldova, and Estonia to secure the fifth position. As expected, Johannes Vetter clinched the gold. Despite not winning, the experience enriched Neeraj. Competing with world champions was itself a significant achievement for him. Although he was the youngest and less experienced, his performance in his very first competition was notable. Competing alongside his idols, Johannes Vetter and Thomas Röhler, was a reward in itself for Neeraj in this premiere event of the Diamond League.

In his first-ever Diamond League event, Neeraj Chopra earned four points, significantly positioning India among the nations that performed commendably. Typically, Indian athletes have limited participation in the Diamond League, though India does have a presence in the medal tally of global athletics championships. However, no Indian had yet made the Indian flag fly in the prestigious arena of the Diamond League. Neeraj was set to end this drought.

In athletics, the Diamond League holds a status akin to the Grand Slams in tennis. This one-day spectacle encompasses 32 athletic events and unfolds across a series from Doha to Zurich, spanning 12 global cities. Athletes earn points based on their performances through the 13-event series, culminating in a final showdown in Zurich. The champion receives a prize of 30,000 US dollars, with monetary awards distributed among the top eight finishers, thus adding a layer of incentive beyond the sporting achievement in each leg of the series.

Neeraj Chopra continues to participate in the Diamond League to maintain and improve his performance consistently. It took him five years to win a medal there, a journey spanning from the Olympics to the Diamond League, inscribed in the annals of time. After his stellar debut in the 2017 Diamond League, Neeraj dazzled at the 22nd Asian Athletics Championships in Bhubaneswar on July 9. Just eight days later, he was off again for the Diamond League, competing in Monaco on July 21. Despite being the youngest competitor, he finished seventh with a throw of 78.92 metres.

Amidst the ongoing Diamond League season, the call for the World Athletics Championships in London was sounded. During this period, Neeraj acquired a new foreign coach. Like with his previous Coach Calvert, Neeraj's rapport with Warner Daniels was excellent right from the start, setting the stage for further successes and international exposure.

Neeraj Chopra had qualified for the World Athletics Championships, a dream for every determined athlete, and particularly significant, as participating in the Olympics and World Championships are major milestones. The Olympics requires a four-year wait, while the World Championships take place every two years. Having missed the chance at the Rio Olympics, Neeraj was eagerly awaiting a medal at the World Championships.

In his first World Championship appearance, Neeraj did not advance past the qualification round. On August 10th, in

London's Olympic Stadium, he failed to meet the 80-metre mark necessary for qualification. Alongside him, Johannes Vetter from Germany delivered an impressive performance, throwing 91.20 metres, asserting his dominance in both the Diamond League and World Championships. Neeraj managed a throw of 82.26 metres, placing him seventh in the qualifiers. As expected, Johannes Vetter went on to clinch the world title in javelin throw. Another Indian competitor, Davinder Singh, also failed to meet the qualifying mark of 80 metres, falling short in his attempt to advance.

Frustrated with not qualifying for the final round in his first World Championship, Neeraj Chopra focused on the final Diamond League event in Zurich on August 24. In his first attempt at the competition, he threw his best distance in the Diamond League series, reaching 83.80 metres, giving his best efforts. Straining his shoulder, he managed 83.39 metres in his third attempt. He attempted another strong throw in the fourth round, which resulted in a foul. Experiencing shoulder pain, he decided not to attempt the last two throws. He finished seventh in the league.

Suffering from a severe shoulder injury, Neeraj had to withdraw from the field. His injury required him to withdraw from the rest of the events in the 2017 season. During this challenging time, his coach, Werner Daniels, provided significant support. Neeraj took adequate rest and followed a nutritious diet to overcome his injury. After a month, he started supplementary exercise sessions at the sports wing of the Indian Army in Vijayanagaram. Once fully recovered, he and Coach Daniels headed to Germany, where Daniels successfully applied biomechanical techniques to improve Neeraj's throwing mechanics, marking a new beginning in his javelin throw career.

Just as a machine performs with greater precision, the application of biomechanics introduced precision in Neeraj's body movements. This approach began to manifest during his training in Germany, significantly transforming his javelin throwing technique. Neeraj started effortlessly achieving throws beyond 85, 86, and even 87 metres. This improvement was not just about enhancing his performance; it was setting the stage for potential gold medals at the upcoming Commonwealth and Asian Games. This phase of training overseas was paving the way for Neeraj to create a new chapter in history, hinting at the heights he was destined to reach in his athletic career.

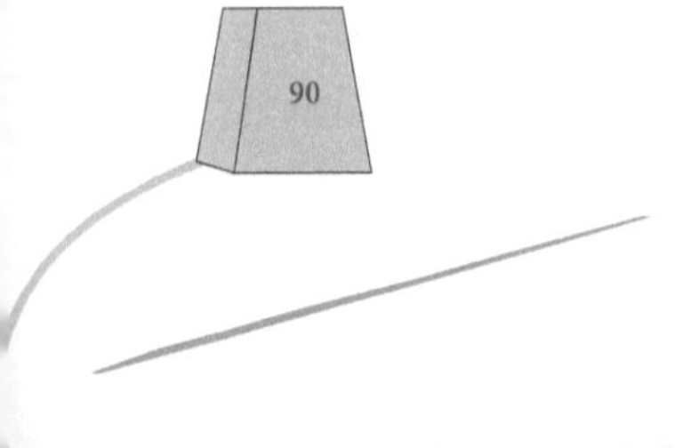

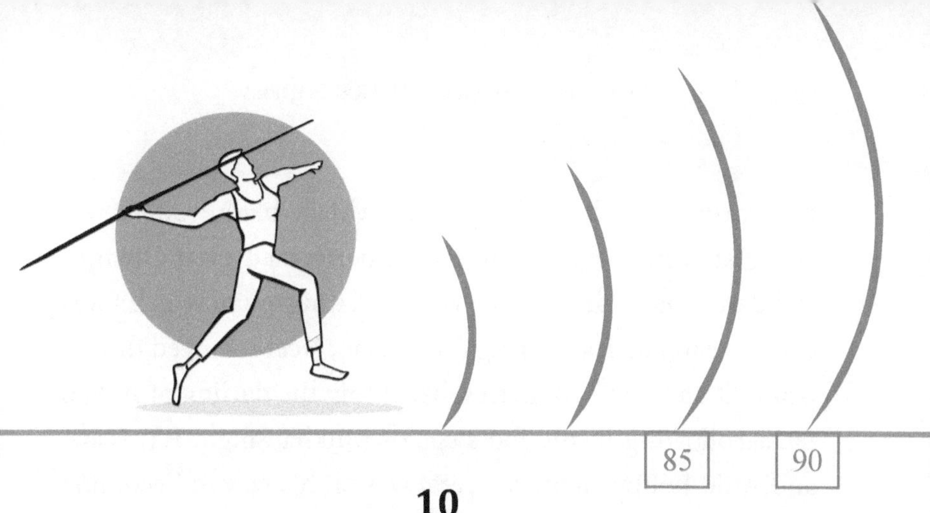

10

Conquered Australia, Indonesia

Foreign Coach Werner Daniels' biomechanical training worked wonders for Neeraj, not only helping him recover from his injuries, but also preparing him to be the finest javelin thrower, not just in India, but across the Commonwealth and Asia. Neeraj's game saw rapid improvements, and he also embraced a new hairstyle, growing his hair long like Mowgli. This reminded many of the famous long-haired style of Mahendra Singh Dhoni, the former captain of India's world champion cricket team. Neeraj, too, unveiled this new look, drawing parallels with Dhoni's iconic style.

The military did not object to Neeraj's growing hair. Typically, all members of the armed forces are required to maintain a short, military-style haircut. However, Neeraj was granted an exemption to this rule. His explosive performance began in February of the 2018 season, which, before 2021, was considered his golden year. He outperformed even Olympic standards that year, a golden record-setting era of which I was a witness in Jakarta. During this season, Neeraj ranged throws from 80 metres to 88 metres, becoming the darling of Indian fans. Following in the footsteps of Milkha Singh, P.T. Usha, and Anju Bobby George, Neeraj was on his way to becoming a contender for Olympic medals and global accolades.

Neeraj's golden year of 2018 began with training in Germany under Coach Werner Daniels, who rigorously mentored him. It was winter both in India and Germany at that time. Despite the harsh cold back home and the snowfall in Germany, Neeraj's training continued uninterrupted. In Offenburg, there were specialized facilities for javelin throwers, including an indoor synthetic track for running and a 100-metre green field for javelin landing. This field was also used for football when not in use for javelin. Neeraj was amazed by this sports facility. Even as snow fell outside, Neeraj was sweating it out on these grounds.

During December and January, the fields of Offenburg became a second home for Neeraj. His training was going on, when Coach Daniels informed him that a javelin throw festival was scheduled for February at the same grounds. World champion Johannes Vetter from Germany had confirmed his participation. Yet, Neeraj was undeterred and registered for the competition. It was a significant opportunity for him, as he would be the first Indian athlete to compete in the Offenburg Javelin Festival, eager to showcase his best performance.

On February 3, 2018, the Javelin Festival was bustling, from the early morning, at the stadium in Offenburg. Dressed in a black tracksuit, Neeraj, sporting his Mowgli look, successfully completed his first throw with finesse. In his second attempt, he hurled the javelin with great speed and force. Just before reaching the final line on the running track, Neeraj's javelin took flight. He executed a leap akin to Hanuman, taking care to not foul as he placed both hands near the ground a few metres before the final line. His throw registered at 82.80 metres, drawing applause from the German audience who admired Neeraj's performance. Johannes Vetter, the seasoned champion, secured the gold, while Neeraj clinched a silver medal. This was the result of two months of rigorous training in Germany. Neeraj was only 1.20 metres short of Vetter's performance. This competition gave Neeraj a new perspective, proving that he could compete with and challenge global athletes.

Many talented athletes falter when faced with world champions, their morale weakened despite having the capability to defeat their opponents, often due to a timid mentality. The nervousness of competing with world champions is visible on the faces of many athletes during international competitions. When the draw reveals that they are in a group with a champion athlete, many athletes find themselves under a lot of stress. Neeraj never backed down from facing his formidable competitor, Johannes Vetter. He continued to showcase his experienced gameplay. This eliminated any fear of playing against world champions from his mind. This was why, even in a javelin throw dominated by European athletes, the Indian flag was flying high with pride.

Upon his return to India after making a mark in Offenburg, Neeraj demonstrated his unmatched prowess at the Indian Grand Prix and the Federation Cup in Patiala, proving that even after five years, he was still the best in the country. During this period, many javelin throwers in India were striving for international medals, and Neeraj impressively stood out from the rest.

As 2018 dawned, India ramped up preparations for the Commonwealth Games and the Asian Games. In April 2018, the 21st Commonwealth Games commenced in Gold Coast, Australia. Athletes from 71 Commonwealth nations, totalling 4,426 competitors, vied for gold, silver, and bronze medals. Indian athletes started celebrating gold medal wins from the first day, ultimately securing 26 golds, 20 silvers, and 20 bronzes, placing India third in the medal tally.

While Indian athletes were seizing gold in shooting, wrestling, weightlifting, and boxing, a drought of gold medals persisted in athletics. Indian athletes were nowhere close to podium finishes in the running events. Though the air was filled with cheers for Indian victories in discus throw events for both men and women, no Indian athlete had managed to secure a gold in athletics even after 10 days into the games.

On April 12, 2018, the men's javelin throw qualification day didn't bring promising results either. Although Neeraj cleared the qualification mark of 78 metres, he ranked second in his group with a throw of 80.42 metres. Pakistan's Arshad Nadeem set a national record with a throw of 80.45 metres, marginally ahead of Neeraj in the final listings. Another Indian, Vipin Kasana, also qualified through the preliminary round.

In the qualifying round, Australia's Hamish Peacock emerged as a potential champion. From the 24 javelin throwers, 12 were vying to become the new champion at the Commonwealth Games. The narrative often echoed Tokyo Olympics—stories of potential winners written early. Julius Yego of Kenya, previous gold medallist from Glasgow and silver medallist at the Rio Olympics, faltered during the qualifiers. Meanwhile, Keshorn Walcott, the bronze medallist from Rio, withdrew from the competition, setting the stage for a new champion in Gold Coast.

On April 13, 2018, the afternoon session sparked fiery competition among javelin throwers from Grenada, Australia, Pakistan, New Zealand, Sri Lanka, Kenya, South Africa, Trinidad, Saint Lucia, and India. Neeraj excelled right from his first attempt. Not only was he on track for a medal, but he also marked a distance of 85.50 metres, setting a benchmark that seemed unbeatable. His precise throw had everyone in awe. For an hour, the best javelin throwers from Australia and Grenada strained every muscle to surpass him, but no one could exceed 83 metres, securing Neeraj's golden throw as the pinnacle. Though his second attempt was a foul, his fourth throw was a season's best of 86.47 metres, firmly planting his flag of victory.

Neeraj ended India's gold medal drought in athletics at the Gold Coast event. He was the only athlete to clinch a gold for the country in athletics at the Commonwealth Games. It was the first time that a javelin throw had secured a gold medal for India in the history of the Commonwealth Games, with the national flag soaring at the highest. Australia and Grenada were the respective silver and bronze medallists.

In the history of javelin throwing at the Commonwealth Games, Neeraj was the second Indian to win a medal.

Previously, his first coach from Patiala, Kashinath Naik, had secured a bronze at the 2010 Delhi Commonwealth Games.

Only five Indian athletes have ever reached the pinnacle of winning a gold medal in athletics at the Commonwealth Games. Milkha Singh brought home the first gold in 1958. In the 2010 Delhi Games, discus thrower Krishna Poonia won gold. The Indian 4x400 relay team also clinched gold in the same event. At the 2014 Glasgow Games, shot putter Vikas Gowda achieved the glory of winning the gold medal. Following these feats, Neeraj Chopra became the fifth Indian athlete to create a golden legacy for the country at the Commonwealth Games.

Neeraj was celebrated nationwide for his double triumph. However, upon returning to India, he immediately began preparations for the Diamond League, bypassing the welcome ceremonies. The season of the prestigious Diamond League was set to start on May 4, 2018, in Doha. The Germans dominated the javelin throw, with the top three spots held by Rohler, Vetter, and Hofmann, who had all thrown beyond 90 metres, establishing the high standard of the competition. Unlike the previous season, Neeraj was no longer behind. He broke his own national record with a throw of 87.43 metres, securing fourth place.

After a promising performance in the Diamond League, Neeraj felt as though he had wings. He continued to compete internationally, placing sixth and fifth in the May and July

Diamond League events, respectively. However, on July 17 in France and on July 28 at the Grand Prix in Finland, Neeraj reached the pinnacle of success by winning gold. Competing against global athletes in international competitions was making him tougher and well-rounded. This period was a test of his physical capabilities. His physique and fitness were developing steadily, akin to those of champion athletes. He was gaining new experiences with each competition, steadily progressing toward global success, undeterred by the elements, as he pursued his Olympic dream.

After his triumphant run, Neeraj received a golden touch from his new foreign coach, Uwe Hohn, a German legend. Hohn significantly contributed to transforming Neeraj into a world-class javelin thrower. Under Hohn's training, Neeraj's technique became more precise, focusing on minimizing small technical errors and aiming for throws close to 90 metres. Hohn was gradually instilling in Neeraj the techniques to reach the world champion level. This German former great javelin thrower was now shaping a formidable athlete from India. Neeraj was being sculpted into a diamond by Hohn.

In the history of athletics, Uwe Hohn is immortalized as the only athlete to throw a javelin over 100 metres, achieving a historic throw of 104.80 metres in Berlin in 1984. This record is still considered the world record. Hohn's incredible throw led to a redesign of the javelin in 1986 to mitigate safety risks and ensure throws didn't exceed the confines of the stadium.

The redesign involved moving the centre of gravity forward to prevent erratic landings and ensure safer competition.

Uwe Hohn of East Germany, who had won the gold medal in javelin at the 1985 World Championships, could not compete in the 1984 Olympics due to East Germany's boycott of the Los Angeles Olympics. After retiring, he decided to fulfil his Olympic dreams through coaching. He coached Zhao Qinggang of China, who won gold in javelin at the 2014 Asian Games. In 2018, Hohn signed a contract with India and became Neeraj Chopra's coach. With Neeraj, Hohn, the Dronacharya of javelin, found his Arjuna. Hohn refined Neeraj's technique. This very technique led Neeraj to intensively train in Finland with Hohn for a month before heading to the Jakarta Asian Games. Neeraj was set to make history, and I was going to witness his feats at the Asian Games.

Under the guidance of the experienced Coach Uwe Hohn, Neeraj delivered a golden performance at the Grand Prix in Finland and then headed directly to Jakarta. Jakarta, the capital of Indonesia, was set to host the Asian Games, considered the Olympics of Asia, a significant event held every four years. This was Neeraj's first Asian Games, where he was to represent India.

Neeraj Chopra's athletic event, as usual, was towards the end of the competition schedule. However, for the Jakarta Asian Games, Neeraj was to participate in the opening ceremony.

He had the honour of being the flag bearer for his country, a distinction given only to champion athletes. Given his gold medals at the World Youth Championships, Asian Athletics Championships, Commonwealth Games, and his potential as a gold medal contender in Jakarta, Neeraj carried the national flag at the dazzling opening ceremony. He displayed the flag at the main athletics stadium, the very field where he was set to compete in javelin. No Indian athlete had previously achieved a gold medal in javelin at the Asian Games. Neeraj was poised to write a new chapter, undergoing rigorous practice sessions in Jakarta.

On the third day of the competition, Neeraj unexpectedly appeared in the wrestling arena. He was there to watch the final match of Vinesh Phogat, the gold medallist female wrestler. Neeraj encouraged and congratulated her, then left slightly late for his practice session in athletics. However, his presence at the wrestling venue sparked rumours of a romance between Neeraj and Vinesh. Earlier at the Gold Coast, Vinesh had attended the athletics stadium to watch Neeraj's gold-winning performance. They even took a photo together, leading many journalists to speculate about their relationship. Neeraj clarified the next day that his visit to the wrestling arena was solely to support a fellow gold medallist athlete. Although Vinesh did not stay to watch Neeraj's event in Jakarta, the gossip about their friendship persisted. The narrative came to a conclusive end when Vinesh married wrestler Somvir Rathi in December 2018.

Neeraj Chopra skipped just one training session in Jakarta to watch Vinesh Phogat's wrestling match. For the next twelve days, he immersed himself in javelin training with Coach Uwe Hohn, aligning himself with the environment at the competition venue. Training at the actual competition venue helps athletes adapt to different atmospheric and environmental conditions, which are never the same as their regular practice grounds. This preparation is crucial for synchronizing with the local conditions and often plays a significant role in securing a win. Arriving in Jakarta 14 days early allowed Neeraj to comfortably adapt without feeling any pressure. He came, he saw, and he was set to conquer Jakarta.

From the moment I arrived in Jakarta, the anticipation of witnessing Neeraj, with his Mowgli-like hairstyle, compete and possibly throw for gold was palpable. Finally, Monday, August 27, 2018, marked that golden day. The evening session was set to showcase the battle among Asia's best javelin throwers at the Carno Stadium. I had pitched my spot right behind where Neeraj would be throwing, just beyond where the Chinese fans, waving their red flags, were seated.

During the Asian Games in Jakarta, the javelin competition started intensely from the first round among athletes from nine countries. Neeraj Chopra, dressed in a blue T-shirt and looking regal, entered the field, bringing joy to us Indians. The competition was fierce with athletes from China, Chinese Taipei, Qatar, Japan, Thailand, Hong Kong, Indonesia,

Pakistan, and India. Right from the beginning, it was clear who might claim victory and who might falter.

Great expectations were set for Chao Cheng from Chinese Taipei, considered a tough competitor for Neeraj. Cheng started strongly in the first round but fell back in subsequent throws. Li Qizhen from China secured a medal early with an impressive throw of 82.22 metres in the first round. Neeraj, grasping his javelin which had a sharp edge with a purple tail and red-yellow colours, made a champion-like entrance and delivered a stunning 83.46-metres throw in his first attempt, setting a high mark in the competition at the Carno Stadium in Jakarta, akin to his performances in the Olympics and Commonwealth Games, declaring, "No one goes beyond me."

No one improved their performance in the second round, and Neeraj's throw resulted in a foul. The third round proved decisive. Neeraj ran with all his might and launched the javelin into the air. It soared, cutting through the air and landing at 88.06 metres, setting a new national record and marking the best performance of his career. I witnessed this moment. This throw surpassed his Tokyo Olympics gold medal performance by one metre, establishing Neeraj's capability to excel beyond historic achievements. Three years before his Olympic triumph, I was fortunate to witness his peak performance in Jakarta.

Before his javelin hit the ground, Neeraj Chopra raised his hand in salute, celebrating his imminent golden victory.

China's Li Qizhen had cleared the 80-metre mark again but was still 6 metres behind Neeraj. Both Neeraj and Qizhen were the only competitors to successfully throw beyond 80 metres. The gold for India and silver for China positions remained unchanged from the first round. However, the bronze medal competition between China and Pakistan was closely contested. Eventually, Pakistan's Arshad Nadeem edged out China's Qizhen by just 29 centimetres with a throw of 80.75 metres.

India's Shivpal Singh was also representing the country. After throwing his first javelin at 74.11 metres, he had to withdraw due to a shoulder injury, but Neeraj had already made history in his debut competition, elevating India's pride.

At the victory podium, the flags of India, China, and Pakistan were raised, with the Indian tricolour flying highest. The national anthem played, creating a spine-tingling moment.

For the first time in the history of the Asian Games, India achieved a gold medal in javelin throw, surpassing the previous best, a bronze by Gurtej Singh in the 1982 Delhi Asiad. Neeraj's gold in Jakarta became a legendary tale. His handshake with bronze medallist, Arshad Nadeem, also showcased the spirit of sportsmanship, marking a notable chapter in the Games.

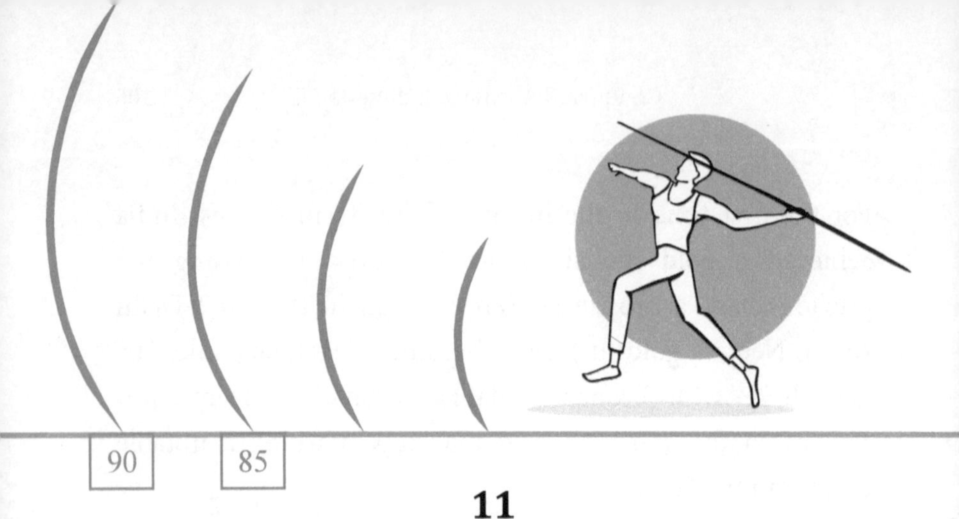

11

Neeraj and I were heroes in Jakarta

For us sports journalists, the Asian Games and Olympics are like celebrating Diwali and Dussehra. During these prime sporting events, just like the athletes, our excitement overflows. In 2018, I had the joy of covering the Asian Games in Jakarta, Indonesia. I spent three continuous weeks immersed in the wonders of Indonesia, witnessing the magical performances of many athletes clinching medals. Seeing the Indian flag hoisted in over 25 venues was a moment of sheer pride. What more could I have asked for?

Covering the Asian Games, Commonwealth Games, Olympics, and World Cups are pilgrimage sites for sports journalists. At least once, we get the fortune to cover these grand stages. I completed this sports pilgrimage during the 2014 Incheon Asian Games, but my thirst was not quenched.

For the second time, similar to covering the Olympics, I had the golden opportunity to report live for News 18 Lokmat channel, thanks to the Indian Olympic Association.

It is a unique experience to interview the remarkable Indian sports icons – Manjeet Singh, dismissed from his job by ONGC, Tejinderpal Singh who cheered for the 'king', Neeraj Chopra who threw the javelin with great confidence, Jinson Johnson who dedicated his medal to the people of Kerala, Swapna Barman who has six toes on each foot, and Hima Das who achieved a hat-trick of medals, late into the night. The thrill of the athletics competitions began in the evening session and the final races would start after eight. This schedule meant that medal distribution and subsequent doping tests kept the interviews with medal-winning athletes available for the channels only after eleven at night, going on until midnight. Being a vegetarian, I often couldn't get dinner at night. However, the joy of interviewing these medal-winning athletes for five minutes was indescribable.

I had to wait until a new day dawned to interview Neeraj Chopra. After midnight, he stood in front of the camera. Despite it being the middle of the night, Neeraj gave me an interview with great affection for News 18 Lokmat. His face beamed with joy as he talked about setting a new record with a gold medal, saying that the training in Finland had paid off. He mentioned that the medal would definitely energize him for the Olympics preparations.

In the interview I conducted, Neeraj Chopra revealed at the end that, like Bajrang Punia, he dedicated his medal to the late Prime Minister Atal Bihari Vajpayee. It was my first meeting with the gold medallist Neeraj. He appeared shy and reserved. He answered the journalists' questions in just a few words. I met Neeraj again for an interview in Tokyo during the Olympics. That interview too took place late at night. The Neeraj I met in Jakarta and the Neeraj in Tokyo were completely different. Over three years, he had become a much more experienced and mature athlete.

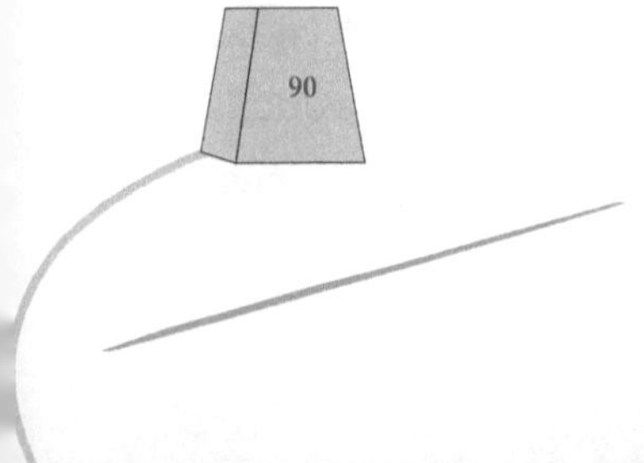

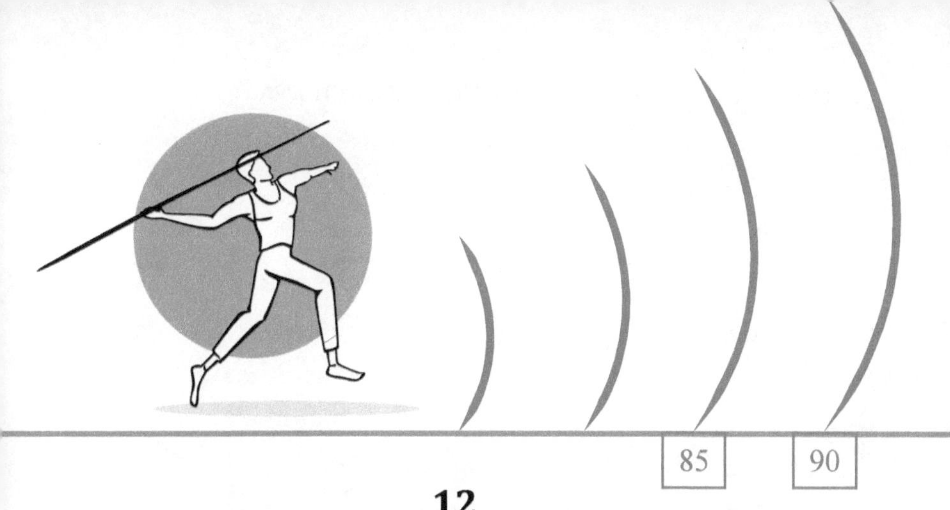

12

J is for Javelin Throw

After Neeraj Chopra threw an 800-gram javelin into the sky and clinched his Olympic success, the fascination with javelin throw as a sport soared across India. This sparked curiosity about how he achieved such precision in his throws. Historically in India, javelins with wooden shafts and iron tips were used on the battlefield. In modern Olympics, men use an 800-gram javelin while women use a 600-gram javelin. The length of the javelin for male athletes ranges from 2.60 to 2.70 metres, and for females, it is between 2.20 to 2.30 metres. Nowadays, Olympic athletes use javelins made of fiberglass or carbon fibre with steel tips.

For practice, Indian athletes can purchase an aluminium javelin for around three and a half thousand rupees. Neeraj's

state-of-the-art carbon fibre javelin costs over 110,000 rupees. He uses four javelins for practice, costing over 400,000 rupees in total. The government has provided Neeraj with 117 javelins and javelin machines, spending 75 lakh rupees, similar to how special bats were crafted for cricket legend, Sachin Tendulkar. This specialized javelin proved perfect for throwing, which was why Neeraj had selected four specific javelins out of hundreds for his Olympic preparation.

Once athletes receive the javelin, they first learn how to grip it properly. There are three main types of grips: 1. American 2. Finnish 3. 'V' grip. Neeraj Chopra uses the 'V' grip, in which the javelin is held such that the middle and fourth fingers form a 'V' shape, similar to the English letter 'V'.

During a javelin throw, the javelin is held parallel to the ground and at the level of the athlete's forehead, creating a stance similar to the English letter 'T'. After gripping the javelin, athletes take approximately 14 to 17 large strides, accelerating into a full sprint.

Javelin throw requires more strength than shot put and more precision than discus throw. It is similar to bowling in cricket, where the object is thrown over the head with one hand while running vigorously. Like in cricket, where stepping over a specific line results in a no-ball, in javelin throw, stepping over the line before the throw is considered a foul. This rule ensures that all throws are made within the designated boundaries to maintain fairness and accuracy in the competition.

Throwing the javelin accurately without committing a foul is a technique mastered through regular practice. During the approach, four steps away from the foul line, three crossover steps are taken diagonally at a 30-degree angle to the right. The final step before the foul line uses the left foot as a brace. The midsection of the body is swiftly thrust forward, and the right shoulder gathers all the strength to propel forward. The momentum from the run-up is concentrated in the last five steps, where the body leans slightly backward. All the energy is then channelled into the javelin throw, which is performed at an angle of 26 to 32 degrees to the ground. During the throw, the entire body, arm, and shoulder lean forward in the direction of the throw, ensuring alignment throughout the motion. It is crucial to approach the resistance line at maximum speed and execute the throw without crossing it to avoid a foul. The last five steps of the run-up should end about two to two and a half metres from the foul line, requiring precise measurement of the approach path.

Expert coaches are essential for javelin throw training to ensure the technique is learned correctly and safely, preventing injuries to the athlete or others. Once athletes have mastered the technique, they are prepared to compete in events.

In competitive javelin throwing, each athlete initially gets three attempts to perform their best. After the first three rounds, the top six athletes get another three chances. Only the longest throw from these six attempts is considered for medal contention. Champion athletes often strive to deliver their best throw right in the first round. However, many javelin throwers have clinched medals by performing excellently in the final round of various competitions.

Javelin throwing can begin from a school-going age. After initially participating in school competitions, athletes qualify for state and national competitions. Competitions for under 14, sub-junior, junior, and open categories are organized annually by athletic organizations. After winning national medals in the junior category, athletes qualify for international competitions. As they progress and improve their performances, they get opportunities to participate in South Asian, Asian, Commonwealth, and Olympic Games. Neeraj started his journey to success from school competitions, ascending through the ranks by winning Commonwealth and Asian medals before clinching the Olympic gold.

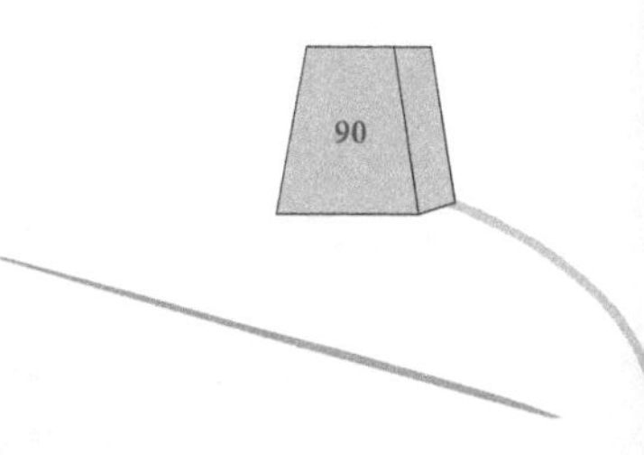

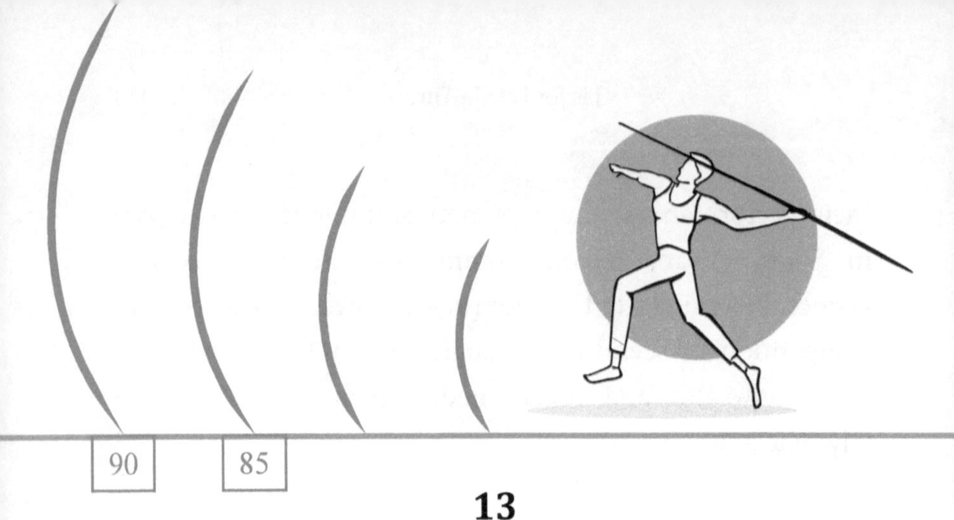

13

Hopping Continents

I witnessed Neeraj's impressive throw of 88.06 metres in Jakarta first-hand. After winning the medal, it was nearly three hours later, around half-past twelve at night, that Neeraj gave an exclusive interview to News 18 Lokmat. He responded succinctly to the questions. The next day, he was scheduled to depart for Zurich. On August 30, 2018, the final showdown of the Diamond League was set to unfold. While all other Indian athletes had returned home, Neeraj alone embarked on this new mission directly from Jakarta to Zurich. He had been competing internationally for over a month and a half, having come from winning competitions in Finland to Jakarta. Back home, everyone eagerly awaited his return, with the military organizing a special reception for him. But for Neeraj, competition was more important than felicitation and so he focused on his participation.

Despite needing rest, Neeraj took the early morning flight from Jakarta for the Diamond League competition in Zurich. When travelling from one country to another, athletes like Neeraj have to carry their equipment, which involves adhering to specific regulations and ensuring all necessary permits are in place. It takes a lot of care to transport long javelins safely from one country to another. Special arrangements must be made to transport javelin equipment at airports, a rigorous process Neeraj is well accustomed to.

When athletes compete on the field, the immense effort behind their performance is often not apparent. After throwing hundreds, even thousands of javelins, a technique is developed. To reach greater distances, the same action must be performed daily with more precision and vigour. Only after thorough practice and safely placing the javelins in their appropriate spots, can the field be left. When travelling to another country, Neeraj had to arrive at the airport 3 to 4 hours before his flight to ensure all his javelins were securely checked in. Only after all equipment was securely stowed could he collect his boarding pass. In Jakarta, he packed his javelins overnight and left at dawn for Zurich to compete in the Diamond League.

In Zurich, Neeraj was the only Indian competing in the prestigious Diamond League. The competition heated up on the evening of August 30th. Athletes from Germany, Estonia, Poland, Czechoslovakia, and Latvia, a country smaller than the state of Maharashtra, fiercely contested. Neeraj, the youngest competitor from India, initially secured the fourth position with a throw of 78.53 metres. Veteran German athlete Andreas Hoffman maintained the lead from the first round, eventually clinching gold with a stunning throw of 91.44 metres in the third round. Meanwhile, Magnus from tiny Estonia secured the second place early in the second round with a throw of 87.57 metres. In the same round, Neeraj reached his best distance of 85.73 metres, moving into third place. Despite not managing a longer throw in the subsequent three rounds, his bronze medal was confirmed by the fifth round. In the sixth round, Thomas from Germany edged out Neeraj by just three centimetres, pushing him to fourth place. Although Neeraj missed a medal by a few centimetres and finished fourth, he was the first Indian to deliver such a top performance in the Diamond League finals. Unperturbed, he left the field with new experiences and soon took off for another country, heading to the Czech Republic for the first time to compete in the Continental Cup.

In the city of Ostrava, Czech Republic, the 2018 Continental Cup was scheduled to take place on September 8th and 9th. Seven Indian athletes had qualified for this event. The competition features teams from four continents: Africa, the Americas, Asia-Pacific, and Europe, and is played in a team format. Neeraj Chopra represented the Asia-Pacific team in this competition. Each team had two athletes competing in the javelin throw, with only the best performer from each team progressing to the final rounds.

Olympic medallist Thomas Röhler from Germany fouled in the first round. In the opening round, India's Neeraj Chopra performed brilliantly, achieving a throw of 80.24 metres, the longest among competitors from Germany, Kenya, Chinese Taipei, the Czech Republic, South Africa, Colombia, and Grenada. In the second round, Thomas, representing Europe, moved into the top spot, pushing Neeraj down to third place. In the third round, Cheng from Chinese Taipei, also representing Asia-Pacific, secured second place with a throw of 82.06 metres. Neeraj's challenge ended when he fouled in the third round.

Thomas Röhler and Cheng maintained their consistency, advancing to the final. In the final round, Thomas secured the gold medal with a throw of 87.07 metres. Due to the team format, only one athlete from each continent could advance to the final, which meant that Jakub Vadlejch from the Czech Republic, despite a strong throw of 84.76 metres, finished in fifth place. Neeraj ended up in sixth place. It was Neeraj's first experience of such a thrilling semi-final and final format in javelin throw. Exhausted from continuous competitions over the past five months, Neeraj was eager to return home. In India, celebrations were waiting for him to honour his achievements, especially his gold medal from the Asian Games. The entire country was eagerly awaiting his return.

Upon landing at Delhi Airport from the Czech Republic, Neeraj was given a grand welcome. The celebrations continued for eight days across Delhi and Haryana. Even after returning to India, his competitive journey did not halt. On September 19, 2018, at the All India Services Athletics Championships held in Jalahalli, Neeraj clinched the gold medal with a promising throw of 83.90 metres.

The National Sports Awards ceremony, originally scheduled for August 29, 2018, on India's National Sports Day, was postponed due to the Asian Games. The ceremony took place on September 26, with President Ram Nath Kovind presenting the awards in Delhi. The Athletics Federation of India had recommended Neeraj alone for the prestigious Khel

Ratna Award. However, he was honoured with the Arjuna Award. In November, Neeraj received more good news: the Indian Army had promoted him to the rank of Subedar.

The year 2018 was a golden period in Neeraj's career. He had proudly hoisted the Indian flag at the topmost position in both the Commonwealth and Asian Games.

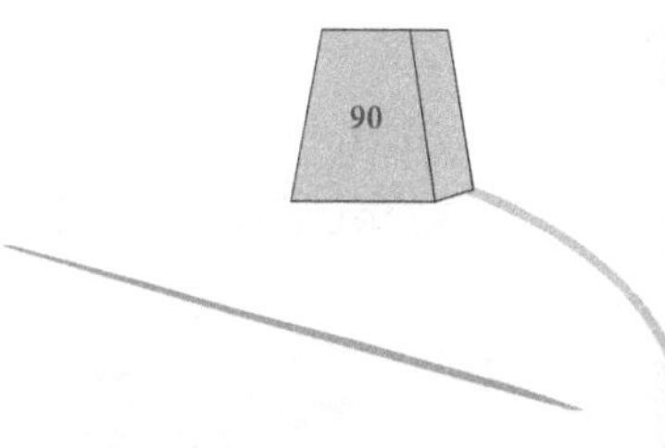

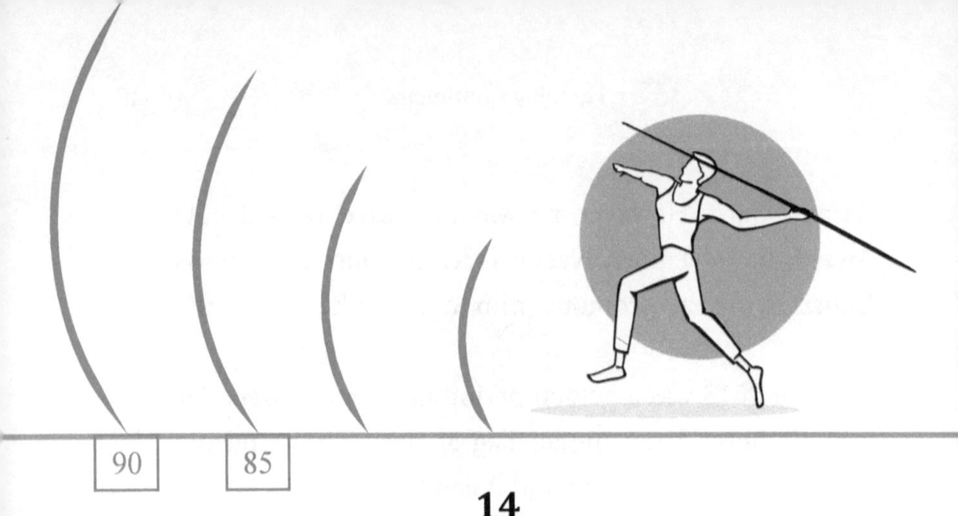

14

Days of Injury

Neeraj's golden, spectacular performance dominated the 2018 athletics season. Throughout the year, he showcased impressive skills in more than 15 competitions. He achieved outstanding results at the Jakarta Asian Games, raising the flag of success high. Travelling internationally, he became an experienced javelin thrower. He played like a machine, running 20 metres and then hurling the javelin with all his might—a skill requiring great expertise. In competitions, he did this not just once but six times, and in practice, hundreds of times. It was exhausting. Neeraj continued this rigorous practice throughout the year.

The human body has its limits, and Neeraj was no exception. At the beginning of the new year in 2019, he started feeling a gradual pain in his right elbow. For a month, Neeraj continued

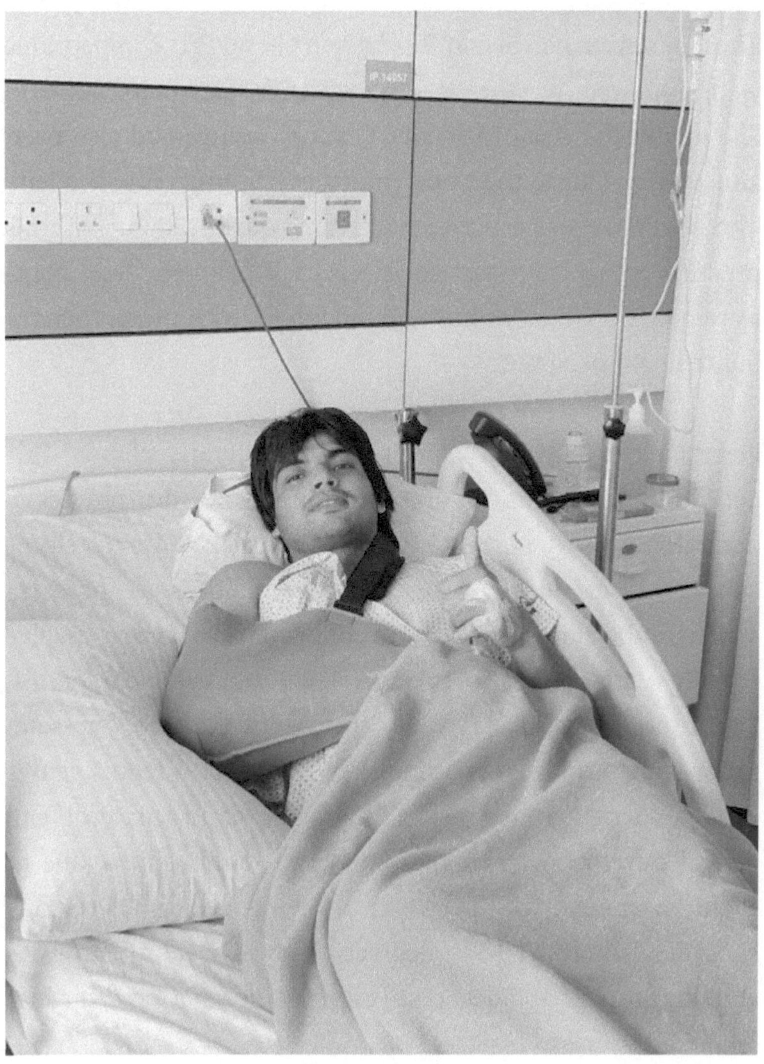

his practice sessions, taking painkillers and seeking help from a physiotherapist. However, by February 2019, the elbow injury had worsened. As the pain intensified, doctors advised him to stop practicing completely.

The new season had begun. The Indian Grand Prix competitions were followed by the World Athletics Championships in Doha, and the Asian Athletics Championships had also been announced. Due to the elbow injury, everything came to a halt. The year 2019 was crucial for Olympic qualification. With his practice completely stopped, Neeraj felt helpless. Treatments were going on, and he was making efforts with physiotherapy, but the pain persisted.

Neeraj experienced a pain similar to tennis elbow. This condition is common among those who do physically demanding work, play racket sports, or cricket. Tennis elbow can also occur in people with weak shoulders, as the extra strain on the elbow leads to this condition. Sports that involve playing with a racket, such as lawn tennis, table tennis, badminton, or cricket, require the use of the elbow muscles for specific strokes, increasing the likelihood of tennis elbow. Overall, excessive use of the muscles leads to this problem. Neeraj developed an injury, similar to tennis elbow, due to the high intensity of his javelin throwing. A normal person's shoulder rotates 80-90 degrees, but a javelin thrower's shoulder rotates 180 degrees. This extreme rotation can cause shoulder injuries.

Neeraj started treatments with several renowned orthopaedic doctors in Delhi, Haryana, and Punjab. However, there was no improvement; the pain persisted. Temporary relief methods included taking painkillers, applying ice, and performing supplementary exercises. March arrived, and his practice had been completely halted for the past three to four months. He was going to miss the world championships, and his career faced the threat of coming to an end.

Sports medical experts advised Neeraj to undergo surgery. However, there was uncertainty about whether he would be able to play again post-surgery. There was a fear that he might have to stop playing altogether. Many legendary athletes have had their careers interrupted by injuries at the peak of their careers. Sachin Tendulkar had also faced the crisis of tennis elbow like Neeraj. From 2004 to 2006, Sachin struggled with tennis elbow. Eventually, after a successful surgery, he returned to the field and continued to score centuries, becoming the master of centuries.

In the past, there were no definitive treatments for tennis elbow in India, so athletes had to go abroad. But now, modern surgeries are also being performed in India. If relief is not found after a few weeks of physiotherapy, steroid injections are administered into the elbow. However, if more than two injections are given within a short period, there is a risk of weakening the muscles and making the elbow unstable. Therefore, it is beneficial to get an MRI and take a single dose of steroids based on expert advice. If still there is no relief, the fibrous tissue knot (Nirschl fibre) is removed through arthroscopic or open surgery.

Injections were not going to stop Neeraj's pain, and surgery was the only solution. There was a debate on whether the surgery should be performed in India or abroad. Commonwealth medal-winning wrestlers, Geeta and Babita Phogat, recommended renowned orthopaedic surgeon Dr. Dinshaw Pardiwala in Mumbai to Neeraj. His sponsors, JSW, also approved of Dr. Pardiwala.

Dr. Dinshaw Pardiwala had successfully treated Olympic medallists Sushil Kumar, P.V. Sindhu, and Saina Nehwal. Therefore, Neeraj made the wise decision to seek treatment from Dr. Pardiwala in Mumbai. At the end of April, he was admitted to Kokilaben Dhirubhai Ambani Hospital. In the first two days of May, various tests, including X-rays, were conducted. It was diagnosed that Neeraj's injury was severe, and his right elbow was locked. This led to the decision to perform surgery immediately.

On May 3, 2019, Dr. Dinshaw Pardiwala decided to operate on Neeraj's right elbow. The surgery lasted two hours. The challenge was to repair the torn tissue in his elbow. Dr. Pardiwala successfully conducted the surgery on the torn tissue. Neeraj shared the news of his surgery along with photos on social media, showing his bandaged arm:

"Undergone elbow surgery in Mumbai
by Dr.Dinshaw Pardiwala. Will require
some months of rehabilitation before

I can start back with throwing.
Hoping to return stronger.
Every setback is a setup for a
comeback. God wants to bring you
out better than you were before.

फिर मिलेंगे. (Will meet again)"

Even though the surgery was successful, the treatment had to continue. Doctors advised Neeraj to engage in supplementary exercises with the help of physiotherapy for the next four months. After taking a week of sufficient rest at the hospital in Mumbai, he went to the IIS Rehabilitation Centre in Karnataka. There, Dhananjay Kaushik began treating his operated elbow. Rehabilitation is as important as surgery. Kaushik gradually helped Neeraj recover from his injury. During this time, Olympic medallist wrestler Bajrang Punia was also undergoing treatment for an injury at Kaushik's centre.

At the IIS centre, Neeraj worked out for two hours in the morning and 90 minutes in the evening. The morning sessions focused on full-body relaxation using medicine balls, cycling, and supplementary exercises. The evening sessions included exercises to enhance the movements of his shoulder and elbow, ensuring that no strain was put on them.

One hundred days after the surgery, Neeraj began exercises that included throwing medicine balls of various weights and throwing sticks weighing 100 grams. He gradually recovered from his injury. He never took a break from his exercises and showed great enthusiasm in his workouts, following every instruction diligently.

Post-surgery, Neeraj also had dietary restrictions. He had to consume the food recommended by his nutritionist, and he never complained about this. He completely avoided sweets, though he occasionally requested for potato chips, which was allowed. For almost a year, he hadn't eaten traditional Haryanvi food. Once, he told his physiotherapy assistant, Ishaan Marwaha, "I want to eat properly just once."

By September 2019, Neeraj had fully recovered and was ready to throw the javelin again. The 2019 athletics season was coming to an end. The World Athletics Championships were set to take place in Doha in October, and Neeraj was eager to participate. He had also confirmed his participation in the National Athletics Championships. However, there was a risk of re-injury if he exerted himself too much. Neeraj decided to seek advice from Adille Sumariwalla, a former Olympian and the president of the Athletics Federation of India. During a routine check-up with Dr. Dinshaw Pardiwala in Mumbai, Neeraj met with Sumariwalla, who advised him that the Olympics were more important than the World Championships. He suggested that Neeraj skip the World Championships and instead prepare for the Olympic qualifiers the following year. He recommended Neeraj train abroad for two to two and a half months to prepare for Olympic qualification.

Neeraj found Sumariwalla's advice to be sound. He made the right decision to skip the World and National Championships and focus on the Olympic qualification round. By then, the countdown for the Tokyo Olympics had already begun. In August 2020, Japan was set to host the grand event. In the new Olympic year of 2020, Neeraj would strive to secure his place in the qualification round.

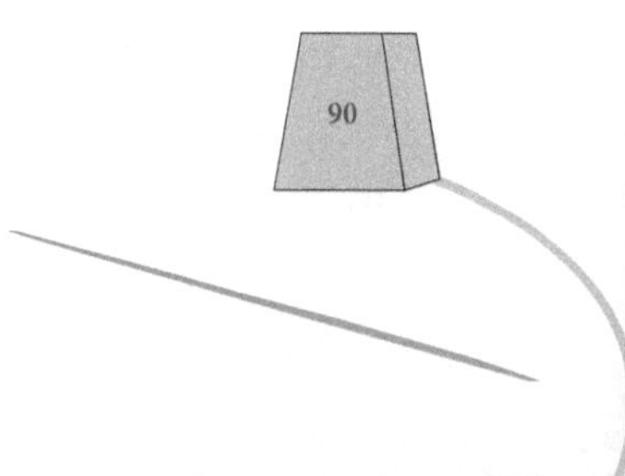

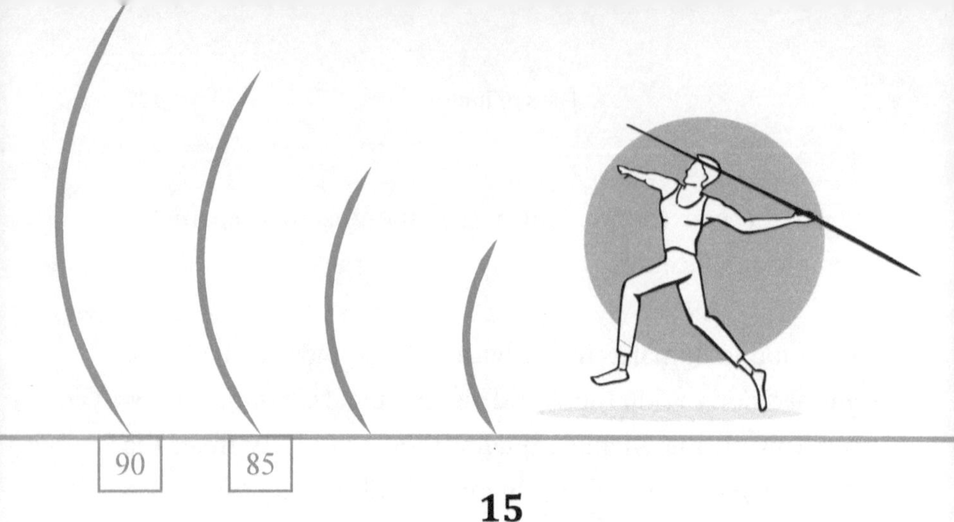

15

The Dark Clouds of COVID-19

After immense, boundless, and unlimited hard work, the dream of winning an Olympic medal begins to take shape. Unlike other world championships, the Olympics do not occur every one or two years. If a chance is missed, there is a long wait of 48 months. After four years of intense preparation, dedicating sweat and effort in the sports arena, the opportunity for an Olympic medal finally smiles upon the athlete.

Since missing out on the Rio Olympics, Neeraj had been eagerly anticipating the Tokyo Olympics. The whole world was preparing for the event. Overcoming his injury, Neeraj resumed his intensive training cycle in November 2019. After practicing in India for a few days, he headed to South Africa with his coach, Klaus Bartonietz. Post-injury, biomechanics

expert Klaus Bartonietz had once again become Neeraj's mentor. The Sports Authority of India (SAI) had renewed Klaus Bartonietz's contract until the Olympics. Foreign coaches had been brought to India to elevate the standards of athletes in various sports and to prepare them for the Olympics. This decision was seen as a promising step toward the country's Olympic success.

With Klaus Bartonietz's vast experience and deep knowledge of javelin throwing, Neeraj started throwing the javelin beyond 80 metres again. During the training sessions in South Africa, Neeraj's performance improved, day by day. He trained with athletes from various countries, which greatly benefited him. Coach Bartonietz had a precise understanding of Neeraj's physique and limitations, and he tailored the training sessions to elevate Neeraj's performance.

Finally, after 16 long months, on January 28, 2020, Neeraj was set to compete in an international event at the Olympic qualifying league in Potchefstroom, South Africa. Having spent a month in South Africa, he had acclimatized to the environment.

In the league competition at Potchefstroom, only five athletes were vying for Olympic qualification, with three from France and two from India. The Indian contenders were Neeraj Chopra and Rohit Yadav. Neeraj, wearing a black tracksuit, made a promising start with his first throw, which landed at 81.63 metres. Neither Yadav nor the three French competitors managed to throw beyond 80 metres throughout the competition, with the French athletes reaching only around 70 metres. In the second round, Neeraj improved to 82 metres, and in the third round, he reached 82.57 metres. However, the Olympic qualification standard was set at 85 metres. In the initial stages of the

Potchefstroom competition, no one had met the Olympic qualification mark.

In the fourth round, Neeraj threw the javelin with full force, achieving a distance of 87.86 metres. The joy on Neeraj's face, along with that of his Coach Bartonietz, was evident. Neeraj had accomplished his second-best career performance and secured his qualification for the Tokyo Olympics. His previous best was 88.06 metres at the Jakarta Asian Games. I was a witness to this remarkable achievement, a testimony to my good fortune.

The plan devised by Neeraj and Adille Sumariwalla to skip the World and National Championships and focus solely on the Olympic qualification event proved successful. Neeraj's throw of 87.86 metres in the qualification was an indicator of his potential to become an Olympic medallist. Many champion athletes reserve their full capacity for the Olympic qualifiers, often skipping significant competitions such as World and Asian Championships for two years or more. Even after securing their Olympic qualification, they refrain from participating in other competitions, focusing solely on the goal of winning an Olympic medal. This decision was particularly wise for Neeraj after his injury, demonstrating his potential as an Olympic champion.

Until February 2020, Neeraj continued his training sessions in South Africa, dedicating himself entirely to javelin throwing.

With the prospect of becoming an Olympic athlete, he trained with increased intensity. In March 2020, plans were made for him to travel to Turkey for further training. However, just as he was preparing to leave for Turkey, he received sudden instructions to return to India. The COVID-19 pandemic had begun to wreak havoc worldwide, leading to lockdowns across the globe. Consequently, Neeraj had to abandon his travel plans and head straight to Delhi, eventually reaching the training centre of the Sports Authority of India in Patiala.

Upon returning from abroad, Neeraj had to quarantine for 14 days as per COVID-19 regulations. On March 21, Prime Minister Narendra Modi announced a complete lockdown in the country. Overnight, the entire nation came to a standstill. Factories shut down, sports fields became deserted, and roads emptied. People were prohibited from leaving their homes unless absolutely necessary, and face masks became mandatory for any essential outings. The coronavirus originating from China was causing chaos worldwide.

Olympic preparations were also affected. As Japan faced its own wave of the virus, there were increasing calls to cancel the Olympics. However, instead of cancelling, the Japanese government decided to postpone the Olympics by one year due to the pandemic.

In March 2020, the entire world went into lockdown. Following the Olympics, various other major events were cancelled, including European football leagues and Wimbledon in England. Athletes, like everyone else, were confined to their homes, unable to train. Many of the world's largest stadiums were converted into quarantine centres for COVID-19 patients. The internationally renowned Shiv Chhatrapati Sports Complex in Pune, once bustling with athletes and sports enthusiasts, now saw long lines of COVID-19 patients.

The pandemic had a severe impact on the sports world. Jobs were lost across the sector, from sports coaches to those manufacturing sports equipment. Many athletes and sports instructors turned to selling fruits and vegetables to make ends meet.

After the 14-day quarantine period in Patiala, Neeraj didn't go home. With strict lockdown measures in place, all travel and transportation were halted. He found himself stuck at the Sports Authority of India's (SAI) sports hostel. Training on the field and accessing the stadium were prohibited. The main gate of the hostel was locked, and Neeraj had to stay there, adhering to COVID-19 guidelines like maintaining social distance and using sanitizers. While many athletes from Delhi and Punjab went home, only a few athletes from Haryana and other states stayed at the Patiala sports hostel. During this time, Neeraj focused on supplementary exercises related to javelin throwing. He worked out morning and evening in the old gym at the SAI hostel to stay fit.

Since going outside and running on the field was not allowed, Neeraj concentrated on running up and down the stairs of the enclosed hall for exercise. With everything in the field locked, he hung onto the door frame of the hall's grill door to strengthen his arms. He continued sessions of jumping in place, doing push-ups, and performing forward and backward push-ups. Since the field was closed for javelin practice, he practiced the action with a ball, throwing it against the wall thousands of times and catching it. He used both his right and left hands for these drills. Neeraj tied a rope between two window points, holding the rope with his hands and balancing his body while stepping on the rope with one foot. He also used a theraband for supplementary exercises, sweating it out rigorously.

Neeraj firmly believes that if you are serious about fitness, you can find new ways to stay fit in any situation. In Patiala, he discovered many new ways to stay in shape and maintained his fitness during the lockdown.

Neeraj, who was always engrossed in practice, now found himself experiencing the lockdown in the afternoons. With javelin training on hold, he had plenty of free time. He spent it listening to music, talking with family members back in Haryana over the phone, and chatting with friends on his mobile. When boredom struck, he enjoyed watching movies on his laptop.

As March and April passed, the lockdown showed no signs of ending. While government offices slowly began to reopen, sports fields, schools, and gyms remained closed. Trapped in the sports hostel during the scorching months of April and May, Neeraj kept fit by sweating it out in the gym. During this time, COVID-19 made its way into the hostel, infecting many. However, Neeraj remained healthy due to his strong immunity. By frequently washing his hands, using sanitizer, and wearing a mask, he stayed clear of the virus. He only left his room to exercise and eat, spending the rest of his time living a solitary life in his room.

Four months without training left Neeraj feeling frustrated. After a month, he obtained special permission to return to his hometown, Khandra, in Haryana. Even in the village, everything was shut down due to the pandemic. Neeraj was given a separate room at home, where he continued his training. Although he preferred working out in a gym, COVID-19 forced him to exercise at home. He maintained his workout routine in his room, focusing primarily on strength training.

After five months of closure from March 2020, gyms and sports fields for international athletes were finally allowed to reopen. However, contact sports like kabaddi, boxing, and wrestling were still not permitted by the government. Sports like athletics, badminton, and archery, which did not involve physical contact, were granted special permission to resume. In August 2020, Neeraj returned to Patiala. Athletes who received the COVID-19 vaccine were allowed to resume training. Neeraj got vaccinated and started his rigorous training sessions again with renewed determination.

It was decided that the Olympics would be held in Tokyo in 2021 without spectators. The training sessions for Indian athletes who had qualified for the Olympics began. With international travel restrictions in place, training abroad was not an option, so athletes worked hard within the country for the Olympics and other international competitions. Neeraj, back on the athletics track in Patiala, was throwing the javelin with more strength and ease, consistently surpassing the 85-metre mark. Meanwhile, in Hyderabad, Rio Olympic silver medallist P.V. Sindhu was training hard on the badminton court. The Indian hockey team in Bangalore was working tirelessly day and night.

This marked the beginning of a new era for Indian athletes at the Tokyo Olympics. Their rigorous training sessions indicated that they were set to make history. Although no one had predicted it, it seemed evident from Neeraj's dedication that he would be at the forefront, proudly waving the Indian tricolour on the athletics field.

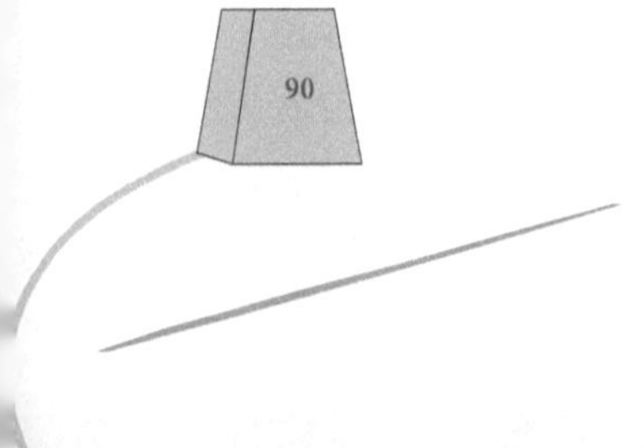

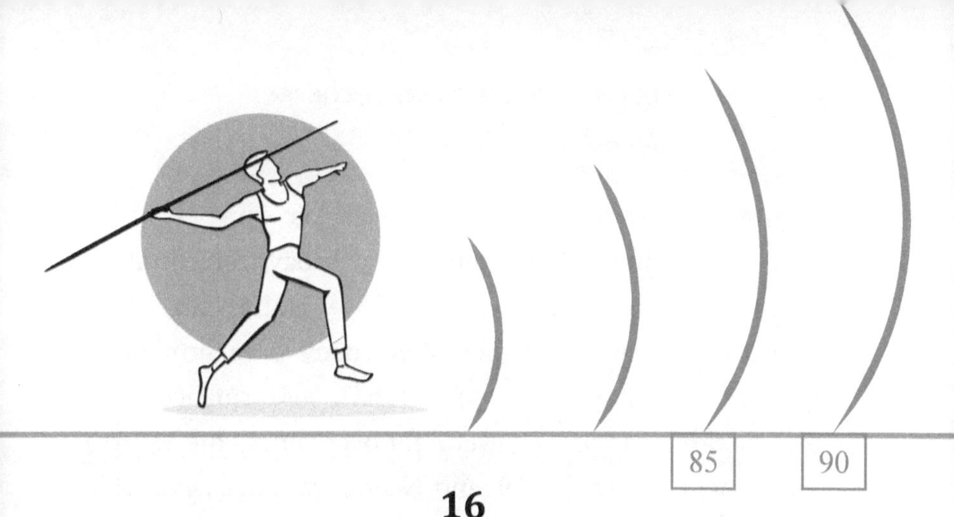

16

The New Olympic Champion

As global COVID-19 vaccination began, the spread of the pandemic reduced. Sporting events started without spectators. After half of 2020 passed, athletes resumed their practice while maintaining social distance. Neeraj continued to train diligently for the Tokyo Olympics, morning and evening. He had prepared to go to Sweden for special training, but his visa was denied due to the COVID-19 case numbers in India. Finally, the Athletics Federation of India planned a training camp in the country itself, after ensuring safe distancing.

The Athletics Federation of India decided to hold a training camp for Indian javelin throwers at Kalaga Stadium in Bhubaneswar from December 2020 to February 2021. With the cooperation of the Odisha state government, the camp commenced, and Neeraj's performance rapidly improved. Along with Neeraj, athletes like Shivpal Singh, Annu Rani, Rajinder Singh, and Rohit Yadav trained under the guidance of foreign coaches Uwe Hohn and Klaus Bartonietz. Training together after many days brought a significant transformation in Neeraj's performance. The three-month camp proved useful for overcoming the adverse environment of COVID-19, and Neeraj was once again able to throw the javelin with vigour. Aiming for a 90-metre throw, he practiced throws ranging from 87 to 88 metres. His performance indicated that he would be a historic Olympic medallist in athletics.

Following COVID-19 protocols, the athletics season in India began in the new year of 2021. After the junior competitions, international athletes were eagerly awaiting the Indian Grand Prix events in the country for Olympic qualification. Due to the pandemic, it was impossible to travel abroad for Olympic qualifying competitions. Therefore, India's potential Olympians aimed to achieve the qualifying times and distances within the country. From February to June, the Indian Grand Prix was to be held in four phases. This competition was the last chance for Indian athletes to qualify for the Olympics. For many of the 16 athletes who qualified for the Tokyo Olympics, the Indian Grand Prix proved to be a boon. Neeraj had completed his Olympic qualification in the Potchefstroom League competition in Africa. He hadn't competed in any event for nearly a year and a half. Thus, he decided to test himself in the third stage of the Indian Grand Prix.

On March 5, 2021, the Indian Grand Prix 3 competition was held in Patiala. Eleven athletes tested their luck, and out of them, only three javelin throwers managed to cross the 80-metre mark. With only a few spectators in the stadium, Neeraj achieved a throw of 83.03 metres in his first attempt. As expected, Neeraj maintained his top position, despite fouling in his second and third attempts. The Olympic qualifying mark was set at 85 metres, but no one had crossed this distance by the fourth round. In the fifth round, Neeraj displayed his brilliance, achieving a throw of 88.07 metres. The announcement over the loudspeakers confirmed it as a new national record. Neeraj had never thrown the javelin this far before, not even at the Tokyo Olympics. Emerging from the challenges of the COVID-19 crisis, Neeraj had accomplished a new feat, signalling to the world that a new Olympic champion from India had risen.

Neeraj's national record sparked discussions across the country, earning him widespread admiration. Just two weeks after setting the national record, Neeraj delivered another promising performance with a throw of 87.80 metres at the Federation Cup competition held in Patiala on March 17, 2021. Initially, he struggled to find his rhythm, but his final throw landed at 87.80 metres. This performance was also superior to his Olympic attempt. Given the consistency in Neeraj's performances, he was considered a strong contender for an Olympic medal.

The Sports Authority of India urgently approved ₹30.85 lakhs for Neeraj's Olympic preparations. His main sponsor, JSW, expressed readiness to provide a support team, including a physio and mental trainer, even abroad. The army, Sports Authority of India, and JSW collaboratively planned "Mission Olympic" for Neeraj. A training schedule and competition timetable abroad were prepared. International flights, halted due to COVID-19, resumed in June 2021. Finally, Neeraj received his French visa and, along with his two coaches and three support staff, flew to Paris.

Due to the COVID-19 situation in Paris, Neeraj had to spend a few days in quarantine. Once it ended, his intensive training sessions began. From Paris, he travelled to Portugal for an international competition, crucial for his pre-Olympic preparation. In his first international season competition, the Cidade de Lisboa event in Portugal, he achieved a throw of 83.18 metres, winning the gold medal. Although he didn't reach the 88-metre mark, his success in the international competition boosted his confidence. On June 19, 2021, Neeraj reached Sweden. While continuing his rigorous training, he also participated in international competitions as part of his preparation. On June 22, 2021, in an international competition in Sweden, he achieved a throw of 80.96 metres, winning the gold. Just four days later, on June 26, he secured a bronze medal with a promising throw of 86.79 metres at the Kuortane Sports Festival in Finland. Neeraj was ready for the Olympics. Completing his final preparation session in Uppsala, Sweden, Neeraj arrived in Tokyo, the Olympic ground.

Amid the deep shadows of COVID-19, the Olympic Games commenced in Japan's capital. Despite the absence of spectators, the grandeur and vastness of the Olympics were not diminished. On July 23, 2022, the Olympic flame was lit. The largest contingent in India's Olympic history was set to compete in Tokyo, with 100 athletes qualifying. Indian athletes were to compete in 16 sports, including archery, athletics, badminton, boxing, wrestling, equestrian, golf, hockey, fencing, gymnastics, rowing, shooting, judo, table tennis, tennis, and weightlifting. The global sports event began the day after the opening ceremony. On the first day of the competition, Mirabai Chanu won a silver medal in weightlifting, raising the Indian flag in Tokyo. Victories began in wrestling, hockey, golf, and boxing, but there was great disappointment in the expected shooting events. The Indian contingent had the highest number of athletes, 24, in athletics. Out of these, 23 athletes did not reach the final round. Neeraj was the sole defender in athletics.

Neeraj was singularly focused on winning an Olympic medal. He had not qualified for the previous Rio Olympics. He was set to make history in his debut at the Tokyo Olympics. While the athletics field saw a series of defeats for Indian athletes during the Olympic events, Neeraj was scheduled to compete in the first qualification round on the morning of August 4, 2021, at 9 A.M.

Thirty-two javelin throwers from around the world were divided into two groups. Neeraj was set to compete among the first 16 athletes in the qualifying round. The top 12 athletes with a performance of 83.50 metres or more would qualify for the finals. Neeraj's first throw in the qualifying round was exceptional, reaching 85.16 metres, securing his place in the final. Among the 16 athletes in the first group, Neeraj was the best.

In the second group, notable competitors included Germany's world champion Johannes Vetter, Czech Republic's Vadlejch, Pakistan's rival Nadeem, and Grenada's Anderson Peters. While Vetter, Vadlejch, and Nadeem managed to qualify, none of them surpassed Neeraj's 85-metre mark. Surprisingly, Vetter, who was widely predicted to be the Olympic champion, did not perform as expected in the qualifying rounds. From the very start, India's flag was flying the highest.

As the sun set on August 7, 2021, the final showdown was set to begin. Out of the 32 competitors, the 12 best javelin throwers qualified for the ultimate battle. These included Neeraj Chopra (India), Weber (Germany), Vadlejch (Czech Republic), Vetter (Germany), Katkavets (Belarus), Nadeem (Pakistan), Mialeshka (Belarus), Mardare (Moldova), Veselý (Czech Republic), Novak (Romania), Etelätalo (Finland), and Amb (Sweden).

Predicting the gold medal winner based on the qualifying performances was challenging. In javelin, the first round consists of three attempts, followed by the top eight of the 12 competitors getting another three attempts in the final round. It was uncertain in which attempt the medal-winning performance would occur. Nevertheless, global commentators predicted that India's Neeraj Chopra was a strong contender for a medal.

Except for the top-ranked Vetter, the players ranked 2 to 6 in the world rankings did not make it to the Olympic final battle. Neeraj was ranked 16th in the world rankings, while the experienced Veselý from the Czech Republic was ranked 26th. In 2021, there were four athletes who had thrown beyond 88 metres better than Neeraj. However, only Vetter qualified for the Olympics. Thus, the final battle for the gold in javelin seemed to be shaping up as Vetter versus Neeraj.

In May 2021, Vetter threw a season-best of 96.29 metres and had surpassed the 90-metre mark six times in the same season. It was obvious who the Olympic champion in javelin would be, without needing a fortune teller. However, Vetter struggled to find his rhythm in the qualifying rounds in Tokyo. In the final, he couldn't perform up to his reputation in the first three rounds and failed to advance to the top eight. In the 2016 Rio Olympics, Vetter had missed out on a medal by just 6 centimetres, with a throw of 85.32 metres, while

Trinidad's Walcott claimed the bronze with a throw of 85.38 metres. Just a month before the Rio Olympics, Neeraj had set a world record with an 86.48-metre throw at the World Junior Championships. However, he missed the Rio Olympics and a chance at a medal as the qualification period had ended.

In Tokyo, Neeraj was ready to make history from the qualifying rounds to the final. He was prepared to shine in the final battle, having already made a mark in the qualifying rounds.

As Vetter's challenge ended in the first three rounds of the final, the stage was set for Neeraj's golden success. The determined Neeraj marked a distance of 86.03 metres in his first attempt and followed it up with a historic throw of 87.58 metres in his second attempt, securing the gold medal. For the first time on the athletics field, the Indian national

anthem resonated, and the tricolour flag was hoisted at the highest point.

I was a witness to that moment, the sight that brought tears of joy to my eyes. India hadn't won a gold medal in the London 2012 or Rio 2016 Olympics. My dream of hearing the Indian national anthem at the Olympics came true with Neeraj's victory. The journey of a farmer's son becoming an Olympic champion was vividly unfolding before my eyes.

Neeraj's performance in the final:
- First attempt: 87.03 metres
- Second attempt: 87.58 metres
- Third attempt: 76.79 metres
- Fourth attempt: Foul
- Fifth attempt: Foul
- Sixth attempt: 84.24 metres

17

Jo Jita Wahi Sikandar

Many athletes, including the legendary sprinters, Milkha Singh and P.T. Usha, had dreamt of winning an Olympic medal in athletics. However, both Milkha and Usha had finished in the fourth place, missing out on medals by mere fractions of a second. Neeraj Chopra erased this painful chapter with his historic performance in Tokyo, overcoming injuries and the COVID-19 crisis to achieve golden success. After winning the medal, he dedicated it to the late Milkha Singh. Prime Minister Narendra Modi personally called to congratulate him, and the entire nation -celebrated.

Neeraj's victory in the Olympics marked a new chapter in Indian sports history, with an Indian athlete emerging as a champion on the global stage. The night before his event, on August 6, Neeraj had felt as if flames were emanating from his body. However, on the night of August 7, after making history, he peacefully slept with the gold medal by his side.

Before the Tokyo Olympics, Neeraj was ranked 16th in the world athletics rankings. After winning the Olympic gold medal, he leaped to the second position. Overnight, by securing the Olympic medal, he climbed 14 places in the rankings. Neeraj scored 1315 points, placing him second in the world rankings, while Germany's Johannes Vetter remained in the top spot with 1396 points, despite missing out on an Olympic medal. Following the Olympics, Neeraj became a prominent name in the global javelin scene. He became India's second "Golden Boy" after Abhinav Bindra. Before returning home with the historic medal, Neeraj was showered with rewards worth crores of rupees. He became a cherished icon among Indian sports fans.

Rewards Received by Olympian Neeraj Chopra

- Haryana Government: ₹6 Crores
- Indian Railways: ₹3 Crores
- Punjab Government: ₹2 Crores
- Uttar Pradesh Government: ₹1 Crore
- Manipur Government: ₹1 Crore
- Board of Control for Cricket in India (BCCI): ₹1 Crore
- JSW Sports: ₹1 Crore

- BYJU's: ₹2 Crores
- Chennai Super Kings IPL Team: ₹1 Crore
- Government of India: ₹75 Lakhs
- Indian Olympic Association: ₹75 Lakhs
- Mahindra: XUV 700 car

Neeraj Chopra became a national hero, receiving numerous accolades and rewards, and he remains a beloved figure in Indian sports.

Neeraj's reward tally didn't end there. Over the year, he received more than ₹30 crores in total, an amount no other Indian Olympic winner had ever received.

After Neeraj's golden success, we Indians celebrated joyously in Tokyo. The entire nation applauded Neeraj. The joy of his victory in the Olympics sounded even in a village in Germany, in Dr. Klaus Bartonietz's village, Oberzschulzenbach. Dr. Klaus Bartonietz had played a significant role in Neeraj's success. The joy of a student's success being celebrated in his mentor's hometown is a rare event, adding a brilliant chapter to Neeraj's success story.

Following his historic achievement, Neeraj was honoured throughout the country. He presented the javelin, which made history at the Olympics, to Prime Minister Narendra Modi in Delhi. The Prime Minister was deeply moved during the meeting. Later, this javelin was auctioned in an e-auction for the Namami Gange project, where it was bought by the

Board of Control for Cricket in India (BCCI) for a whopping sum of ₹1.5 crores.

Neeraj's journey from an aspiring athlete to an Olympic champion has become a shining example of dedication and success, inspiring countless others. His achievements and the subsequent accolades he received have made him a national hero and a symbol of excellence in Indian sports.

Due to the Olympics, the national sports awards were delayed, but Neeraj was honoured with the prestigious Major Dhyan Chand Khel Ratna Award by the President. In 2022, he was also awarded the Padma Shri and the Param Vishisht Seva Medal in recognition of his Olympic achievements. The Indian Army promoted him to the rank of Subedar.

In his birthplace, Khandra village in Haryana, a grand procession was held in Neeraj's honour. His medal was displayed in the village temple for all the villagers to see, and the entire village celebrated the day like a fair. After returning from Japan, Neeraj fell ill due to the constant honours and felicitations. After taking complete rest for a few months, he was set to prepare for the new season. The World Athletics Championship gold medal in 2022 was his next goal.

Neeraj resumed his training sessions on October 20, 2021. As 2021, overshadowed by COVID-19, came to an end, Neeraj continued his rigorous training, aiming for the 90-metre javelin throw in the new year of 2022. In June 2022, at the Paavo Nurmi Games in Finland, he set a new national record with an 89.30-metre throw, earning a silver medal, a performance worthy of his Olympic achievements. His historic Olympic gold-winning throw was 87.58 metres, and with this two-metre improvement, he established himself as a contender for international and world medals. On June 30, 2022, Neeraj shone again at the Diamond League's Stockholm meet with an unprecedented 89.94-metre throw, winning a silver medal and breaking his own record within a month. The world celebrated his achievement, his Olympic gold had catapulted him to the pinnacle of fame overnight. He received an overwhelming number of rewards and honours upon returning from the Olympics. Despite the fanfare, Neeraj remained focused on his training and exercise, never growing tired of his daily regimen. His successes in Finland and Sweden were a testament to his dedication. Now, he had his sights set on the World Championships in the USA.

In Eugene, Oregon, the global athletics festival took place. On Sunday, July 24, 2022, as the sun set in the USA and rose in India, Neeraj's javelin battle began. Having reached the finals, I woke up at 6 A.M. to watch Neeraj's performance. He struggled to find his rhythm in the first round, with his initial attempt resulting in a foul. In his second attempt, he threw the javelin 82.39 metres, and in his third attempt, he improved to 86.37 metres. With determination, Neeraj threw the javelin 88.13 metres in his fourth attempt, leaping to second place. This throw proved to be the turning point, earning India its first-ever silver medal in the history of the World Championships. Anderson Peters from Grenada won the gold with a throw of 90.54 metres. Neeraj became only the second Indian to win a medal at the World Championships, after Anju Bobby George, who won a bronze in the long jump in 2003. Neeraj surpassed this achievement, ending a 19-year medal drought and proving himself as a true Olympic champion.

In August 2023, the World Athletics Championships for the new season were held in Budapest, Hungary. Neeraj was considered the dark horse of the competition. He once again emerged victorious, surpassing formidable competitors from Germany, the Czech Republic, Pakistan, the USA, England, Australia, and Japan.

In the final battleground of javelin throw, Neeraj achieved a golden feat with a throw of 88.17 metres in his second attempt. His traditional rival, Arshad Nadeem, amazed everyone with a promising throw of 87.82 metres. Just two years after the Olympics, Neeraj conquered the summit of the World Championships. He became the first Indian athlete to win a gold medal at the World Athletics Championships. His performance in the qualification round of this championship was also the best of the season, securing his qualification for the 2024 Paris Olympics. Neeraj's triumph resonated throughout the country once again. The entire nation is now focused on the Paris Olympics, hoping to see Neeraj add another historic Olympic medal to his illustrious career.

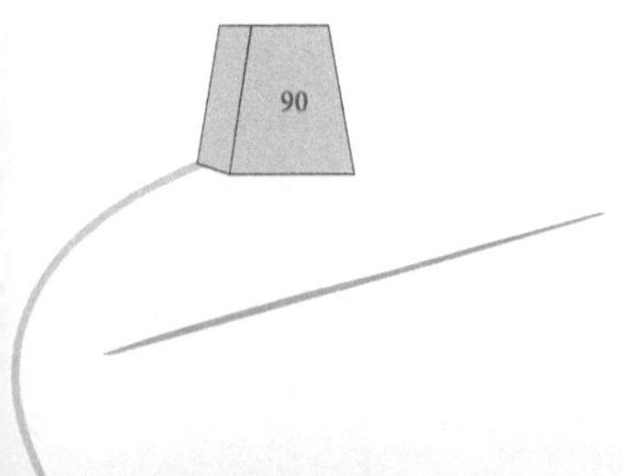

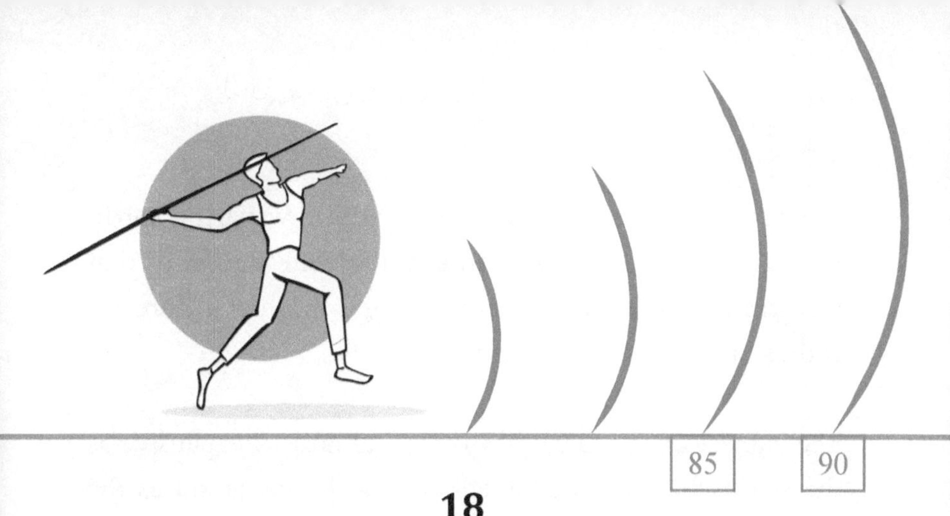

18

Tokyo's Golden Experience

"Crown the winners with the unfading branch,
and make the body worthy and ironlike."

These profound lines from the Greek Olympic hymn resonated through Tokyo on August 8, 2021, during the closing ceremony of the Olympics. My mind drifted back a day, to the very field where the dawn of India's golden era had begun. I was a witness to that historic moment of Neeraj Chopra's golden throw, an event that marked a new chapter in India's Olympic history.

The memory of Neeraj's throw, which secured India's first-ever gold medal in athletics, remained vivid. His triumph was not just a personal victory but a moment of immense national pride, symbolizing the culmination of years of dedication, hard work, and unwavering spirit. Standing in the Olympic stadium, I felt the weight of that historic moment and the promise of a brighter future for Indian sports.

The subject of the Olympics is vast, almost as expansive as the sky itself, and its competitive aspect is as grand as the Mahabharata. However, even a drop of water from the sacred Ganges is said to bestow immense blessings. I was fortunate to participate in the Olympic Kumbh Mela for the third consecutive time after London and Rio. In this global sports congregation, India made historic achievements, clinching 1 gold, 2 silver, and 4 bronze medals. This was India's best performance in the 125-year history of the Olympics. I had the privilege of witnessing six out of these seven medal ceremonies first-hand. Hearing the national anthem on the Olympic podium after Neeraj Chopra's victory filled me with immense pride.

Travelling to Tokyo for the Olympics amidst the COVID-19 pandemic was nothing short of a divine challenge. From the moment I set foot in Tokyo, I faced numerous challenges. During this time, my school friend Ajay Dhake and his friend Rahul Bapat came to my rescue like guardian angels. If they hadn't provided me with a SIM card in time during my quarantine, my live reporting would have been disrupted even before the Olympics began. The dream of covering the Olympics for the third time would have remained unfulfilled if not for their timely help.

Braving the dense fog of the COVID-19 pandemic, my unforgettable experience at the Tokyo Olympics began. July 24, 2021, marked the first day of Mission Olympic and brought a silver medal for India. The petite Mirabai Chanu won the first medal in weightlifting. We hurried to the Tokyo International Forum Stadium, and the sight of Mirabai's silver medal instantly erased all our fatigue. A woman from Manipur, who used to gather wood, had performed a miracle by winning an Olympic medal. She had established India's dominance in the traditionally male-dominated sport of weightlifting. I congratulated Mirabai in Manipuri with *"Khuremjari!"* (Greetings!). The first day Gof the Tokyo Olympics became a medal day for the country, thanks to Mirabai's silver success.

At Mirabai Chanu's press conference, there were only two Indian journalists present, and I was very fortunate to be

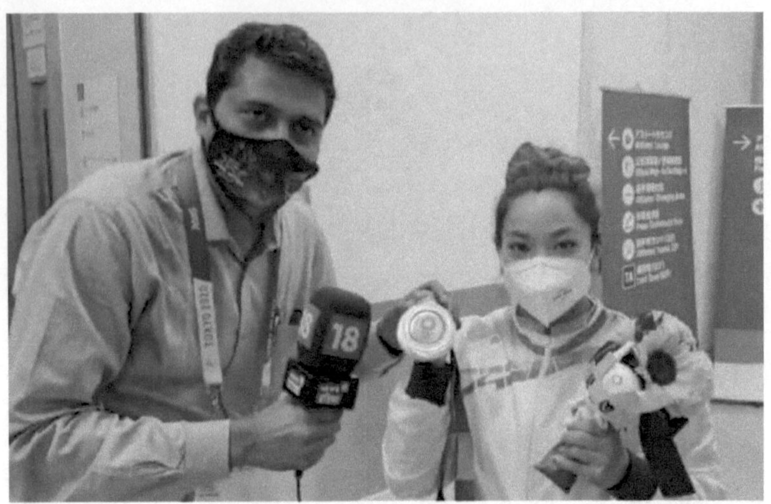

one of them. I conducted an exclusive interview with her for News18 Lokmat. Within moments, my interview with her was broadcasted worldwide. Throughout the day, I appeared alongside Mirabai on News18 Lokmat, News18 India, and CNN News18, as well as on Malayalam and Gujarati news channels.

With high hopes that young world champion shooters would secure the first medal for the country, all journalists and officials from the Indian Olympic Association headed to the Asaka Shooting Range on the day Mirabai won her medal. However, Rahi Sarnobat, Manu Bhaker, and Saurabh Chaudhary all faced deep disappointment. It was hard to believe that Saurabh, who excelled in the qualifiers, failed in the final test. As daily defeats unfolded in the shooting arena, performance post-mortems began right there in Tokyo. The shooters' bag remained empty in Tokyo, just as it had in Rio.

In consecutive Olympics in Athens, Beijing, and London, shooting had been India's pride. But now, this honour had shifted from shooting to badminton. At the badminton court in London, Rio, and now Tokyo, Sindhu kept the tricolour flying high from the very first round. Due to an easy draw in the group stage, Sindhu advanced smoothly to the knockout rounds. Her roar shook Tokyo in the quarterfinals. She defeated the host player Yamaguchi and stormed into the semi-finals for the second consecutive time. However, the fierce Chinese Taipei player Tai Tzu Ying stopped Sindhu's march. The dream of seeing Sindhu win gold faded. But in the historic battle for the bronze medal, Sindhu maintained her reputation. By defeating Chinese opponent He Bingjiao, Sindhu secured her second Olympic medal, making her the first Indian woman to win two Olympic medals. Witnessing Sindhu's historic battles and medal ceremonies in Rio and Tokyo still gives me chills. The tricolour, proudly displayed on both courts, was a testament to the country's rich sports culture.

Before Sindhu's double medal success, the tricolour was already set to fly high at the Kokugikan Sumo Stadium in Tokyo. Lovlina Borgohain secured India's second medal in boxing by winning her second bout. On July 30, 2021, the joy on the faces of Indians was evident. Coming from a hardworking family in Assam, Lovlina didn't have the same glamour as Mary Kom. Her game had been stalled for several months due to an injury. The 69 kg weight category was included in the Olympics for the first time, and Lovlina seized the opportunity. Lovlina became the first female boxer from Assam to achieve such a feat in the Olympics. While the spotlight was on super mom Mary Kom in Tokyo, Lovlina's name was not as familiar.

Lovlina competed in the 69 kg weight category. In her Olympic debut, she defeated Chinese Taipei's Nien-Chin Chen, a former world champion, who had defeated Lovlina multiple times before, including at the 2018 World Championships. Lovlina avenged her previous losses and secured her place on the medal podium. She admires the styles of boxers like Mike Tyson and Muhammad Ali but has developed her own unique style through hard work and determination.

Mirabai Chanu and Lovlina Borgohain from Northeast India earned esteemed positions for India in the Tokyo Olympics

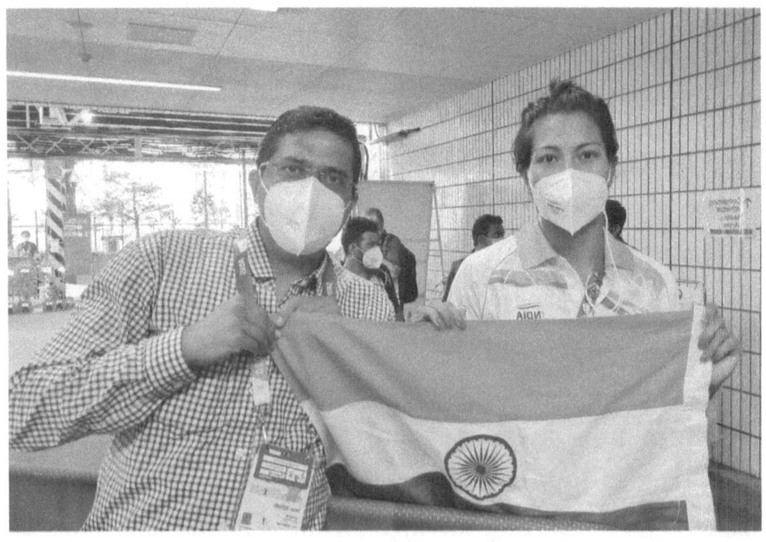

medal tally. Both athletes share a common background, coming from poor families where their next meal was uncertain. They turned this hunger into their strength and made history in Tokyo.

Lovlina preserved the honour of the Indian boxing team. Although she lost in the semi-finals, she still brought home a bronze. Vijender Singh won a bronze at the 2008 Beijing Olympics, and Mary Kom did the same at the 2012 London Olympics. Lovlina's sincere response in my interview—"Every time we reach up to the bronze medal, we stop. This time, I wanted to win gold… a medal is a medal, but I wanted gold,"—brought tears to our eyes, highlighting her unfulfilled dream.

In the Tokyo Olympics, India ultimately secured a gold medal. I was a witness to that golden moment. Many asked me which of the seven medals was the best. My answer, the bronze medal in hockey, raised many eyebrows. Despite Neeraj's golden success, the bronze won by the 14 hockey players felt like a crowning achievement to me.

Having witnessed the dismal performances of the Indian hockey team in London and Rio, I didn't expect miracles in Tokyo either. However, the dynamic young captain Manpreet Singh breathed new life into the team, and goalkeeper Sreejesh's impregnable defence was a significant advantage.

The Indian team's start in the group stage was shaky. After a hard-fought 2-1 victory against New Zealand, Australia handed India a crushing 7-1 defeat. It seemed like it was all over, a repeat of the same disappointing performance. But the Indian hockey team rose from the ashes. They defeated Spain, Argentina, and Japan, advancing to the quarterfinals. There, they stunned Britain with a 3-1 victory, securing a spot in the semi-finals.

Watching the semi-final clash between India and Belgium was a reminder of the thrill that hockey can offer. Despite the experienced and powerful Belgian team defeating India, the match hinted that the Indian team was ready to reclaim its place on the victory podium.

I will never forget August 5, 2021. The match between India and Germany was a visual treat and ended a 41-year Olympic medal drought for India. With a historic 5-4 victory, our hockey players triumphed on the Olympic stage. Seeing the Indian hockey team win an Olympic medal was a dream come true for me. Witnessing this dream turn into reality, I abandoned my journalistic duties and celebrated the historic victory by dancing and singing in the stadium.

The first quarter ended with Germany leading 1-0. In the early minutes of the second quarter, India equalized with a goal, making it 1-1. However, Germany quickly scored two more goals, taking a 3-1 lead. Just as it seemed India might lose, they made a remarkable comeback before the end of the first half, levelling the score at 3-3.

With a promising 5-4 scoreboard, Indian captain Manpreet Singh received a red card. A crucial defender was out, and in the last 20 seconds, Germany earned a penalty corner. But the solid wall of goalkeeper Sreejesh blocked the goal, sparking celebrations across the country. This triumph was more thrilling than any movie, like Shah Rukh Khan's "Chak De India." Our dedicated hockey players proved that dreams do come true. This success was the result of a decade of hard work by Hockey India, the support of foreign coaches, and the unprecedented unity of experienced and new players. After many years, everything aligned perfectly, and the world heard the resounding boom of India's medal win in Tokyo.

In the wrestling arena of Tokyo, our wrestlers continued the tradition of securing medals, though none were gold. The tricolour has consistently had a presence at the wrestling mats in Beijing, London, Rio, and now Tokyo. For the third consecutive time, I had the privilege of witnessing the Indian flag fly high at the Olympic victory podium. This time, Ravi Kumar Dahiya clinched a silver medal in wrestling. He put up a fierce fight against the two-time world champion Zavur Uguev, who eventually won 7-4. Despite his defeat, Ravi made history by becoming the second Indian wrestler to win a silver medal, following Sushil Kumar's achievement in 2012.

While Neeraj Chopra was making golden history on the athletics field, Bajrang Punia secured the sixth medal for India in wrestling. Bajrang won a bronze medal through the repêchage round, raising the country's honour. Simultaneously, Neeraj's javelin throw turned the Tokyo Olympics into a golden moment for us Indians.

...And That Moment Arrived!

It was a golden dawn for Indian athletics. None of Neeraj's competitors could surpass his 87.58-metre throw, and he was declared the champion. With his javelin throw, Neeraj clinched Olympic gold. In the 125-year history of the main Olympic stadium, where only athletics events are held, the tricolour had never been hoisted before. Legendary sprinters Milkha Singh and P.T. Usha had come close, finishing fourth. Milkha Singh had always wished to see the tricolour fly high in this main stadium. Neeraj, emotional during his interaction with us journalists, said, "Milkha Singh taught us to play with all our heart and soul. He should have been here today, but wherever he is, I hope he is watching this success."

India won its first Olympic gold in 13 years with Neeraj's victory. Before Neeraj, shooter Abhinav Bindra had secured India's first-ever individual gold medal. Neeraj became India's second "Golden Boy," earning praise from around the world.

> **India's Historic Performance at the Tokyo Olympics:**
> - **Neeraj Chopra** - Gold (Javelin Throw)
> - **Mirabai Chanu** - Silver (Weightlifting)
> - **Ravi Dahiya** - Silver (Wrestling)
> - **Men's Hockey Team** - Bronze (Hockey)
> - **P.V. Sindhu** - Bronze (Badminton)
> - **Lovlina Borgohain** - Bronze (Boxing)
> - **Bajrang Punia** - Bronze (Wrestling)

Indo Banzai Chants in Japan

Monday, August 9, 2021, the second day after the conclusion of the Tokyo Olympics. It was just morning in India. At that time, in the land of the rising sun, Japan, the mid-afternoon air was filled with the chant, "*Indo Banzai,*" which means, "*Jai Hind,*" or "Victory to India." The sacred Renkōji Temple in Tokyo resonated with chants of "Netaji Subhash Chandra Bose *ki jai,*" and "*Vande Mataram.*" Young Indians paid homage to the statue of Netaji Subhash Chandra Bose, recalling his memories on the occasion of *Kranti Din* (Revolution Day). It was 9 A.M. in India, while Japan was celebrating *Kranti Din* in the afternoon.

On News18 Lokmat channel, the headline "Live from Tokyo: Celebrating August *Kranti Din*" flashed. The whole world was watching my program, witnessing this display of patriotism live. We celebrated the August *Kranti Din* of 2021 at the

Renkōji Temple in Tokyo, sanctified by the ashes of Netaji Subhash Chandra Bose.

I felt immensely fulfilled celebrating *Kranti Din* in the presence of Netaji's ashes, witnessing Neeraj Chopra's golden medal victory at the Tokyo Olympics, and the historic bronze triumph in hockey. These moments were a testament to India's spirit and resilience.

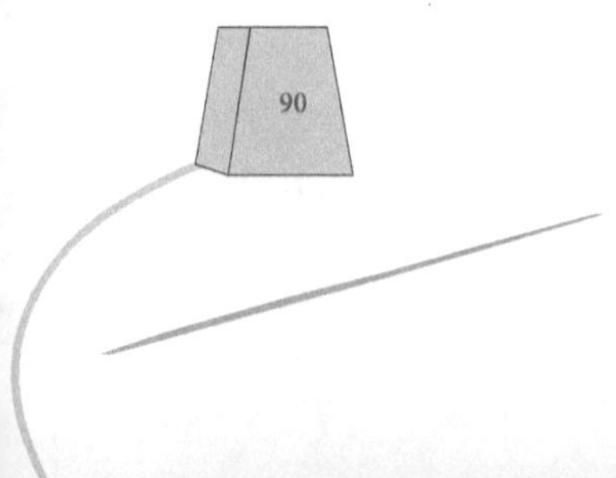

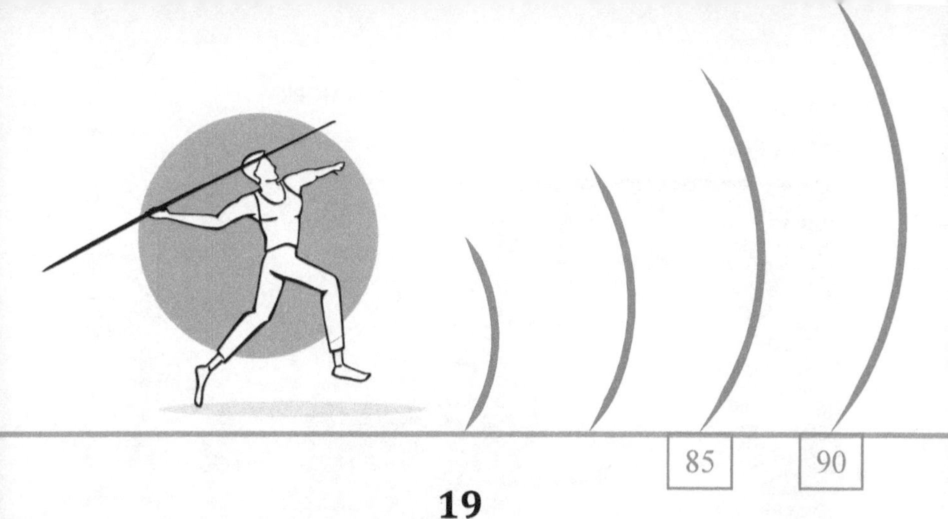

19

The Making of the Golden Boy

From Panipat to the historic medal at the Tokyo Olympics, Neeraj Chopra's journey was marked by precise guidance, expert coaching, family support, school cooperation, and international training with foreign coaches. Additionally, he benefited from timely employment, government assistance, support from the Indian Army, sponsorship from JSW, and prestigious sports awards. All these factors combined to shape Neeraj into a world champion athlete at the age of 24.

Neeraj made the bold decision to pursue a career in sports during his school years, and his family fully supported him. He received excellent coaching from discerning trainers at the Haryana Sports Academy from the very beginning. As soon as he became a national champion, doors opened for him at the national training camp of the Sports Authority of India (SAI).

After achieving international success, he accepted a job offer from the armed forces at the age of 19. Following his remarkable performances in the Asian and Commonwealth Games, the JSW Company sponsored him. The support he received from the armed forces, SAI, and JSW during the challenging phases of his career turned fruitful under Neeraj's determination. The timely assistance from Prime Minister Narendra Modi's Mission Olympic Podium scheme also played a crucial role in the success of Neeraj and other athletes, like Mirabai Chanu and Bajrang Punia, in becoming Olympic champions.

Neeraj continued to build an exemplary character befitting an Olympic champion. His rigorous eight-hour daily training regimen, supplementary exercises to enhance performance, diet, and assistance from physiotherapists and psychologists formed the foundation of his success.

Neeraj does not like to consume high-fat foods in his daily routine. On the day of a competition, he prefers to eat only salads and fruits to maintain his energy levels and avoid feeling heavy. For breakfast, Neeraj eats brown bread and an omelette every day. For lunch and dinner, he eats grilled chicken, grilled salmon, and eggs. When he feels hungry, he likes to drink fresh juice, which he often consumes during training. Recently, he has included salmon fish regularly in his diet.

Talking about his favourite foods, Neeraj loves vegetable biryani and omelettes, which he can eat anytime. He enjoys eating *pani puri* as fast food, believing that the high water content in *pani puri* does not significantly impact an athlete's health. Regarding his cheat diet, he indulges only once every 20 days, preferring to eat homemade *churma*, but he strictly avoids desserts in his daily routine.

Neeraj has a hobby of bike riding and enjoys a specific type of Haryanvi music called Ragini. He is not interested in watching TV and rarely enjoys movies, perhaps once a year. For him, the field practice is his enjoyment.

When Neeraj returned to his homeland after winning a medal at the 2018 Incheon Asian Games, his long hair had become a distinctive part of his identity. However, this hairstyle was not seen at the Tokyo Olympics. Like former Indian cricket team captain, Mahendra Singh Dhoni, Neeraj also loved his long hair. But for the Tokyo Olympics, he decided to cut it. The discipline instilled in him by the armed forces was evident in Neeraj during the 2021 Olympics. He appeared more mature, a complete and ideal athlete.

It's customary to interview medallists at the Olympics. After receiving his gold medal, Neeraj attended a press conference in Tokyo with Czech athletes Jakub Vadlejch and Vítězslav Veselý, where I was also present. Journalists from around the world asked Neeraj questions in English, and he answered them in Hindi. Indian journalists then translated his answers into English for the global audience. The world witnessed Neeraj's love for his mother tongue as he made history.

Before and after the Olympics, Neeraj attended many interview programs. When TV anchors and interviewers asked questions in English, he calmly answered in Hindi. If the program was in India, Neeraj would lovingly ask the interviewer, "You understand Hindi, right? Then ask in Hindi." Olympic champions from Japan, China, and South Korea never speak in English; they always communicate with journalists in their native languages. Neeraj not only elevated the nation's pride by winning an Olympic medal but also honoured the widely-spoken Hindi language by continuing to speak it even after his victory.

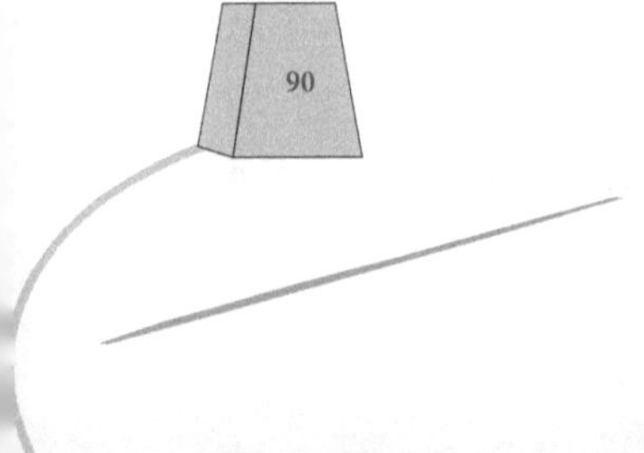

20

Life Journey

Name: Neeraj Chopra

Nicknames: Golden Boy, Nijju

Birth: December 24, 1997, Panipat, Haryana

Mother's Name: Saroj Devi

Father's Name: Satish Kumar

Education: Graduate, D.A.V. College, Chandigarh

Occupation: Subedar, Indian Army, 4 Rajputana Rifles

Sport: Javelin Throw, Athletics

Olympic Performance

Gold: 2021 Tokyo Olympics

World Performance

Gold: 2016, Bydgoszcz, Poland - World Junior Athletics Championships

Silver: 2022, Eugene, USA - World Athletics Championships
Silver: 2022, Sweden - Diamond League
Gold: 2023, Budapest, Hungary - World Athletics Championships

Asian Performance

Silver: 2016, Vietnam - Asian Junior Athletics Championships
Gold: 2016, Guwahati - South Asian Games
Gold: 2018, Jakarta - Asian Games
Gold: 2017, Bhubaneswar - Asian Athletics Championships

Commonwealth Performance

Gold: 2018, Gold Coast - Commonwealth Games

Awards

- Arjuna Award, Government of India, 2018
- Vishisht Seva Medal, Indian Army, 2020
- Major Dhyan Chand Khel Ratna Award, Government of India, 2021
- Padma Shri Award, Government of India, 2022
- Param Vishisht Seva Medal, Indian Army, 2022

Achievements

- **July 26, 2013**: 69.66 metres, Patiala, India
- **August 17, 2014**: 70.19 metres, Patiala, India
- **December 31, 2015**: 81.04 metres, Patiala, India
- **July 23, 2016**: 86.48 metres, Bydgoszcz, Poland
- **June 2, 2017**: 85.63 metres, Patiala, India
- **January 28, 2020**: 87.86 metres, South Africa

- **March 5, 2021**: 88.07 metres, Patiala, India
- **June 30, 2022**: 89.94 metres, Stockholm, Sweden
- **August 28, 2023**: 88.17 metres, Stockholm, Sweden

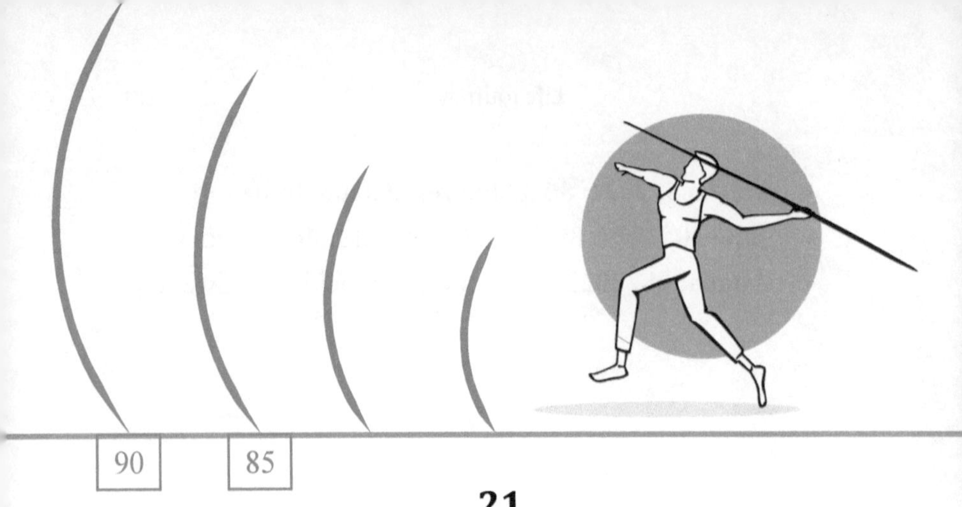

21

India's Olympic Medals

Year	Sport	Athlete	Medal
Paris 1900	Athletics	Norman Pritchard	Silver
Paris 1900	Athletics	Norman Pritchard	Silver
Amsterdam 1928	Hockey	–	Gold
Los Angeles 1932	Hockey	–	Gold
Berlin 1936	Hockey	–	Gold
London 1948	Hockey	–	Gold
Helsinki 1952	Hockey	–	Gold
Helsinki 1952	Wrestling	Khashaba Jadhav	Bronze

Year	Sport	Athlete	Medal
Melbourne 1956	Hockey	–	Gold
Rome 1960	Hockey	–	Silver
Tokyo 1964	Hockey	–	Gold
Mexico 1968	Hockey	–	Bronze
Munich 1972	Hockey	–	Bronze
Moscow 1980	Hockey	–	Gold
Atlanta 1996	Tennis	Leander Paes	Bronze I
Sydney 2000	Weightlifting	Karnam Malleswari	Bronze
Athens 2004	Shooting	Rajyavardhan Rathore	Silver
Beijing 2008	Shooting	Abhinav Bindra	Gold
Beijing 2008	Wrestling	Sushil Kumar	Bronze
Beijing 2008	Boxing	Vijender Kumar	Bronze
London 2012	Shooting	Gagan Narang	Bronze
London 2012	Shooting	Vijay Kumar	Silver
London 2012	Badminton	Saina Nehwal	Bronze
London 2012	Boxing	Mary Kom	Bronze
London 2012	Wrestling	Yogeshwar Dutt	Bronze
London 2012	Wrestling	Sushil Kumar	Silver
Rio 2016	Wrestling	Sakshi Malik	Bronze
Rio 2016	Badminton	P.V. Sindhu	Silver

Year	Sport	Athlete	Medal
Tokyo 2020	Weightlifting	Mirabai Chanu	Silver
Tokyo 2020	Boxing	Lovlina Borgohain	Bronze
Tokyo 2020	Badminton	P.V. Sindhu	Bronze
Tokyo 2020	Hockey	–	Bronze
Tokyo 2020	Wrestling	Ravi Dahiya	Silver
Tokyo 2020	Athletics	Neeraj Chopra	Gold
Tokyo 2020	Wrestling	Bajrang Punia	Bronze

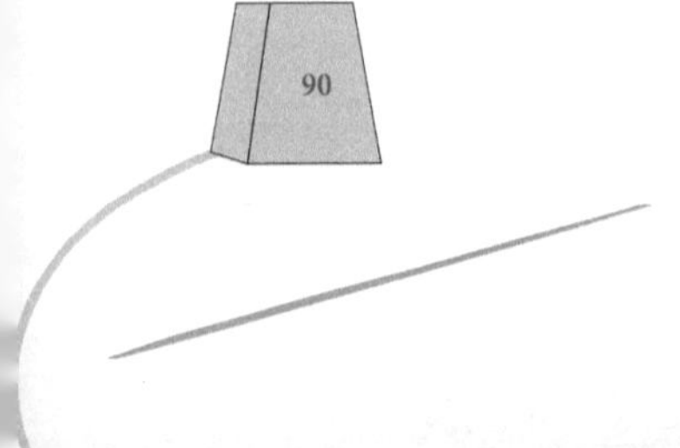

Author Profile

Sanjay Pandurang Dudhane has over 25 years of experience in sports journalism, sports promotion, and sports dissemination. He has been active in sports journalism since 1996, publishing more than 1600 articles in major newspapers in Maharashtra, including 'Sakal.' Dudhane has edited the Diwali magazine 'Ashtapailu' and has hosted programs on Pune and Kolhapur All India Radio. He has provided live coverage for 'News 18 Lokmat' and 'TV 9 Marathi.'

Dudhane is the only Marathi sports journalist to have experienced six Olympic Games, covering the London Olympics (2012), Rio Olympics (2016), and Tokyo Olympics (2021), among others. He has also reported on the Indian cricket team's England tour (2011) and various World Cup tournaments.

He has published several books, including works on Khashaba Jadhav, Sachin Tendulkar, Major Dhyan Chand, Milkha Singh, Mary Kom, and more. His contributions have earned him prestigious awards like the Shahu Maharaj Award (Maharashtra Government), Parshuramiy Sports Award, and Ideal Sports Journalist Award (Maharashtra State Journalists Association).